GILBERT & GEORGE

THE RUDIMENTARY PICTURES

1998

MILTON KEYNES GALLERY
8 OCTOBER 1999 – 9 JANUARY 2000

GAGOSIAN GALLERY, LOS ANGELES
3 FEBRUARY – 11 MARCH 2000

Published on the occasion of the exhibition
Gilbert & George: The Rudimentary Pictures
Milton Keynes Gallery
8 October 1999 – 9 January 2000
Gagosian Gallery
3 February – 11 March 2000

© 1999, Milton Keynes Gallery, Gagosian Gallery and authors
Edition 4000
ISBN 0 9536755 0 5
Editor Stephen Snoddy
Design and production Axis Design, Manchester
Printed by Pale Green Press
Font Helvetica

Milton Keynes Gallery
900 Midsummer Boulevard
Central Milton Keynes
MK9 3QA
England

Tel + 44 (0) 1908 676 900
Fax + 44 (0) 1908 558 308
E-mail – mkgallery@mktgc.co.uk
Website – www.mktgc.co.uk

Director Stephen Snoddy
Administrator Katharine Sorensen
Exhibitions & Admin. Asst. Natasha Messenger

Gagosian Gallery
456 North Camden Drive
Beverly Hills, California 90210
USA

Tel + (310) 271 9400
Fax + (310) 271 9420
E-mail – info@gagosian.com

Directors Candy Coleman, Robert Shapazian
Exhibition Co-ordinators Ealan Wingate, Lisa Kim, Pippa Cohen, Melissa Lazarov

Front cover: *Spell of Sweating*, 1998 (detail)
Photo p. 61 courtesy, English Partnerships

Milton Keynes Gallery gratefully acknowledges financial assistance
from Milton Keynes Council and Southern Arts.
Registered Charity No 1059678

GILBERT & GEORGE

with

David Sylvester

I Tell You Where There's Irony In Our Work: Nowhere, Nowhere, Nowhere.

We are an artist

David Sylvester: Your exhibition at the Ville de Paris [1997] is your first full-scale retrospective, but the show you had in Bologna last year was already something of a retrospective, and I wonder whether you learned anything by seeing it.

GILBERT: Yes, we did learn something. We learned that we would like to make a much bigger one.

GEORGE: We always say that when we see our works together in that way, which is quite rare, we see how similar our development is to the viewer's life, compared with the normal development you see when you see an artist's retrospective: you see his stylistic development; you see how he changes his shapes or his technique. Whereas the viewer has a life's development: you're fifteen and you're scared; you're sixteen, you have sex; you're seventeen, you go to college; you have a life story. And our story in the pictures is similar to the viewer's. It's not a stylistic development, it's a content development.

DS: Well, it is a stylistic and technical development too.

GEORGE: Serving the content. It's not form for form's sake, it's form for meaning.

GILBERT: Form to make it more powerful, form to make the pictures speak louder, form to make it in some way more aggressive. We always like the image to absolutely shout out at the viewer as much as we are able to arrange it. That's why we are teaching ourselves different techniques for manipulating the images all the time. That's why we would never have assistants, because they wouldn't know how to manipulate an image. They would make them all the same, but we are able to increase their power.

GEORGE: The idea is always to make pictures that will form all of our futures a little bit. We want life to be different as a result of our exhibitions. We want people to be affected by seeing the pictures. We want them to go home and be different.

DS: When you say people, you don't actually mean just the usual art audience?

GILBERT: We mean every single person that lives outside there. Every child, every granny, everybody, black, white, Chinese, everybody. Because we don't believe that art is anything else than speaking to the viewer. It's not making aesthetics for an élite.

DS: You're the opposite of avant-garde artists in that sense. Because avant-garde art is tied up with the notion of making esoteric statements.

GEORGE: We don't feel we have to make a comment on art, and we don't even believe that we show life or reflect life, which is what a lot of people think we do. They think our art is somehow related to reality. We don't think that. We think our pictures are about future possibility.

GILBERT: It is all based on inner feeling. It is looking inside ourself. We never look at the world. We always try to feel the inside of what is inside our self. That's the window for the world. To look inside.

GEORGE: People very often say: 'Oh, but you must get your inspiration from somewhere, you must go to young people's clubs or you must travel or something'. And we say we just go out of the door in the morning, it's raining and there's a pool of vomit there, and there are pigeons pecking away at it, there's a matchstick with a little bit of groundsel growing beside it; everything is in there anyway. There is nothing that is not in that immediate scene. And all of those things are also inside a person, and all over the world.

GILBERT: And I must say that all our art in the end is based on the desperation of life. It's very difficult to live. It's very difficult to survive.

GEORGE: It's the second most difficult thing in the world, isn't it? And if you remove the culture, then it's totally impossible. If you go to a city where there's no gallery, there's no public library, there's no concert hall, no university, you need a bodyguard and there are dead bodies in the street.

DS: Do you want to bring that desperation out or do you think it comes out anyway?

GILBERT: Yes, it is unavoidable. I don't know, maybe we are unhappy people. I don't know if everybody else is very happy. I never felt happy. There are some small moments of happiness, but in general it's miserable. If people look at our art from the beginning to the end, it's in some way based on that, that kind of desperation.

DS: You began as a pair of tramps, in Underneath the Arches.

GEORGE: Precisely. We like it very much, we like the words of the song.

GILBERT: It's very interesting. Did you read in Lynn Barber's interview that she went to Dartington to find out what George was like at school, and found out what George said when he was young and was asked what he wanted to be.

GEORGE: I've forgotten it now.

GILBERT: He wanted to be a 'super-tramp'.

GEORGE: I'd forgotten that… Apparently I said that.

GILBERT: And I think that's exactly right.

DS: When you started working together, was it a totally instinctive and emotional thing that brought you together or was it that you'd already formulated similar attitudes?

GEORGE: Well, we don't believe in similar attitudes in that way. I think it was a combination of love at first sight and of circumstances.

We were already working together before we were even conscious of it. It was something that happened to us, we believe, rather than something we decided. We very often think, even when we're making designs for new pictures, it's as though something else has guided our hand to make the design. 'Did we really do that? Who made us do that? Who made us say this?' We do believe in something over ourselves, outside of ourselves, some power. If not we wouldn't do pictures like that. We wouldn't consciously do Naked Shit Pictures. We are dragged into it in some way.

GILBERT: We didn't actually know, but it was some kind of friendship that I always said began because George was the only person who accepted my pidgin English.

GEORGE: I think we came together because we were both apart from the crowd at St Martin's. We weren't goody-goody students, we weren't angling for a teaching job, because we knew we'd never get one anyway; we weren't angling for an Arts Council grant to get a studio, because we knew we wouldn't get one anyway. We knew we could never become the normal good student and we accepted that and made it a quality rather than a handicap. We didn't want to be the good student. We knew they were naive, not us.

GILBERT: So we helped each other. I think that is still what is there. I think that we are only total when we are together.

GEORGE: And also we should remember that we both realised the limitations of that

formalistic art at St Martin's. We saw that all of those sculptures the other chaps were doing could not be taken outside the front door of St Martin's, that they would cease to live in that moment, they would become invisible to those thousands and thousands of fantastic people from all over the world who walk up and down Charing Cross Road.

DS: It was rather like a stroke of fate that not only put you together in the same place, but also organised it so that the place was St Martin's, where there was a certain corporate spirit and a certain complacent formalism. I imagine that that was a marvellous aggravation to you both.

GEORGE: I'm sure that's true. It set us apart in that way.

GILBERT: But it was very exciting. We liked it. In fact we felt on top of the world. We felt we were arrogant artists, who knew exactly where we were going, and we thought that all these formalistic sculptures were total nonsense. And I think that the biggest luck was that we were able to remove ourselves from the art for art's sake.

GEORGE: We fell out of love with art and fell in love with the viewer. I think that was the magic moment.

DS: And when did that happen?

GEORGE: I think that it really crystallised at the moment of leaving St Martin's, because we were so crazy and so separate at that moment. We went to the Tate Gallery and said that we would like to present a crib, as they didn't have a crib at the Tate at Christmas time. We said we would get some sheep from the RSPCA and a donkey and we would stand there and be like Mary and Joseph. A fantastic living piece, with the straw on the ground and everything; we could arrange a little star of Bethlehem. They wouldn't do it, but it was an amazing idea. Still would be amazing, don't you think?

GILBERT: Because we realised that the world was waiting for some kind of art. We were not too conscious that we were doing it, but then we had this idea out of the blue that we were it. We became some kind of object. Like we went to St Martin's holding our sculptures like a ball and a stick, and that's it. Like George was holding a stick and I was holding a ball. Two people make a composition. One person doesn't.

GEORGE: One person looks like a bloody silly artist. We always said that two persons removed self-doubt. We can never have self-doubt. Because the normal artist is always asking himself questions, he is sitting in front of the canvas saying, 'Should I put another green cow in the corner, should I change the colour of the sky?', and no answer comes back. Whereas with two people you've always got an answer. Self-doubt is vanishing. As long as the other one always says yes – and we always say yes to each other. I think we share an enormous sense of purpose. I think that's our greatest strength. We are more concerned with that than with any details.

GILBERT: You know, I don't think we are interested in anything else. I have no other passionate interests. I have no interest in money, or anything. So in the end it becomes very easy to concentrate totally on this vision.

GEORGE: We can be alone together, I think. That's the best thing. Whereas you can't be alone with friends. We don't impose on each other. Therefore we can be alone like a person is alone.

GILBERT: I mean we can be alone with some friends, but very few, and if not you always feel people want something from you, and at that moment you are not free.

GEORGE: They want something from you all the time. And then you get drunk, you cannot relax. You can only relax with a very few people. Your great good fortune – though it's a very trying thing also and it makes great demands – is working with the person that you're attached to personally. It can be enormously rewarding, and it's also enormously difficult. But it solves a lot of problems if you can manage it, though it also creates problems.

GILBERT: We accepted that from the beginning.

GEORGE: Our shared sense of purpose is more important than any of the other details of life. The other things don't matter really. If we can make Shitty Naked Human World, what the fuck else really matters? We are so proud that we can do a picture like that. Incredibly proud. When we see people

standing in front of that picture and chatting amongst themselves, we feel enormously rewarded, because without us they wouldn't have that experience.

DS: Your partnership has lasted much longer than most working partnerships.

GEORGE: We never worked together, that's the important difference. We never collaborated. All those partnerships you think of, it's one person doing one thing and another doing another, bringing their different talents to bear on something. We don't think we're doing that. We never see it that we are doing a picture together in that way.

GILBERT: That disappeared a long time ago.

GEORGE: It disappeared the moment two or three people had said of us: 'Oh, it can never last, because two people can't possibly work out'. We became very determined.

GILBERT: We needed each other. We needed each other because we were not total.

GEORGE: We don't think we're two artists. We think we are an artist.

To make a frozen moment of feeling

GILBERT: We invented a technical form to make our art that doesn't distinguish between us. You don't see the brushstrokes, the hand-written message that every artist is so proud of. We always said that we wanted to make pictures that shoot from the brain like a laser beam.

DS: But I must say that at Bologna I loved those early drawings in which you do see the hand-written message.

GEORGE: You would.

DS: I already loved them back in the early 1970s, but I always thought of them then as drawings of extraordinary poetic delicacy and charm, but, when I saw them in Bologna, I realised they were more than that. It wasn't just this poetic atmosphere they created; it was also the graphic style – that, as in a van Gogh drawing, they achieved a transformation of the natural world into a kind of handwriting, they had this quality of transforming everything into signs made with charcoal.

GEORGE: Quite coarse, though.

DS: Coarse, yes, but very forceful, and a marvellous total transformation. There was no illustration there, there was a re-creation of what was seen in terms of drawing, in terms of marks on paper. So this makes it all the more curious that you insist that you hated it and wanted to get rid of it. But now I've seen why, because of your remark that only one person can make a drawing, only one person can make a particular mark, and you wanted to get away from that.

GEORGE: Yes, and we also wanted to get away from the compliments that we'd had from the viewers – that they loved the technique, they loved the surface, the marks. We had thought we were busy making pictures which were saying something to the viewer, not saying something about charcoal on paper.

DS: Yes, but I think that that is true of a lot of good art, that the art comes unconsciously. I don't think artists make good marks by trying to make good marks. That would be just the way not to.

GEORGE: But we didn't like that they didn't say 'how sad and lonely!' when they looked at the picture. That's what we wanted them to think.

Forever we will search... from, 'The Nature of our Looking', 1970 348 x 246 cm / 137 x 97 ins

GILBERT: When we did the drawings, we had already done photo-works. The first one was in 1969, it was George the Cunt and Gilbert the Shit. That was the first of these rude words, calling ourselves names. We loved that piece. I think that was more the real G & G. Then we did the living pieces. Then it became very difficult: you do a living piece and then what do you do? You can't be in every gallery at the same time. We wanted to leave something behind in the galleries, instead of having to be there all the time. So we thought: how could we arrange a G & G atmosphere? So we said: 'Let's do these drawings, let's make drawings that look like we didn't do them, that already existed'. Like drawings that maybe already existed a hundred years before. In a way we wanted to take away the 'artisticness' that looks like a modern drawing. We wanted to make them look like we found them in a box.

GEORGE: You know those great documents with a red seal on them that you get in local museums – charter from 1620, with a ribbon in it, with a frayed edge, burnt a bit. We wanted them to look like that. Official.

GILBERT: We found them like the Dead Sea Scrolls or something. I mean we found them and that's it.

GEORGE: Charters. Documents. Visual letters.

GILBERT: Again, we wanted to take away the hand.

DS: The drawings are made up of pages from sketchbooks. Did you both work on the same notebook sheet, or was each individual sheet done by a single person?

GILBERT: No, but we put the pages together into the piece that we wanted. We stuck them together with brown paper into a piece like two metres by three metres.

DS: While you were actually working on them?

GILBERT: No, first.

GEORGE: And we had the negative image in our hand, the hand that didn't have the charcoal. A squared-up image.

GILBERT: We did them extremely fast, two to three hours each. Both, over on top of each other we were doing them.

GEORGE: Just to finish them. We had no interest in the actual doing of them.

GILBERT: But then we didn't like them new, so we stained them with buckets of –

GEORGE: – permanganate. Screwed them up even, ironed them out afterwards. As you said, to make them look as though they'd always been there.

DS: And if you'd had the techniques then that you later evolved, those drawings would have been done as photo-pieces?

GEORGE: Yes. If we'd then had the technique and the financial resources.

DS: When you started doing the drinking pieces, the first ones were not on a grid.

GEORGE: They were in different shapes. Shaped as a person, shaped as a rectangle, shaped as a circle, an oval, shaped as something falling, shaped as a swastika,

finally finding our way. It took us many years to end up at a traditional rectangle.

GILBERT: But at that time, 1972, '73, I think that drunkenness took over and that's why we did the drinking pieces. We had money for the first time and we did a lot of drinking, a lot of partying.

GEORGE: We used drinking as the subject and content. We had artist chums at that time drinking with us and then they would get up the next morning and make these appaling, abstract, cool, sober pictures. We thought that was unfair and unrealistic and dishonest. Why not use drink as the subject? Everyone is drunk, everyone understands drunkenness, even countries that don't have alcohol still have other forms of drunkenness.

GILBERT: And I am saying that alcohol took over our lives in some way and made us very desperate. That's why we had titles like Imprisoned. We had those. Then we did Dark Shadow, the book that you know.

DS: As you said, the drunkenness began because you had the money to drink?

GEORGE: Yes. As students we were extremely well-behaved in that sense. We didn't discover bad behaviour at all. We were very grown-up.

DS: I was most drunk when I was seventeen and finished up most evenings lying in the

gutter in Soho. I'm ashamed to say that later I lost my taste for extreme drunkenness.

GEORGE: You did it very young compared with us.

GILBERT: George never lost that. I lost it, because I saw George so drunk, and in that moment I became sober. From that moment I cannot get drunk. When I see George very drunk it's terrifying. I'm terrified of death, of accidents. Two or three or four times he was locked up in prison for being too drunk. Even I ended up in prison. I was the first one.

GEORGE: You went to prison first, and I said to you: 'How ridiculous, you don't know how to handle the police. A gentleman would never be taken into a cell and have the door locked. You must have mishandled everything very badly'.

DS: Besides the drunken pictures you also did in the early '70s a number of photo-pieces such as the Dead Boards series – a series that has always very much moved me through the way it records the human figure behaving in certain ways in space.

GEORGE: It is more the person being dragged at ever increasing speed toward the grave, rather than a technical thing to do with space.

DS: You're not trying to convey the sensation of a human figure walking in space, rather like a Giacometti figure?

GILBERT: I think that what we have in all the pieces, from the beginning to the end, is this

Destructivism, 1972   159 x 197 cm / 62.5 x 77.5 ins

image of people standing still, as still as possible in the world. Frozen. Not too much walking. We want them frozen for ever. In all our images we have that. We have these images of us, people, human beings, who have been frozen. Because only when they are frozen can you look at them. If they start running you cannot look at them. We want to make them more and more still, and more and more that you can actually look at them. You can look inside them. That's why we put paint on our heads when we did the Singing

Sculpture, so you could actually come near and look at us. And that's what we are doing on the new pieces.

GEORGE: We want to be able to freeze thought in a way, to stop the watch, to make a frozen moment of feeling. Because we say if you walk across London Bridge in the morning, you'll probably pass a thousand people, but you won't be able to describe one single person. But if somebody stops you and takes your arm, and says, 'Excuse me, I want to say something to you', you will

remember that for years, maybe for ever. It's much easier to remember a picture than reality. We have said to students at St Martin's, 'How many trees are there in the Charing Cross Road?', and everyone said, 'Ah, trick question, there are no trees'. If you go out in the street there are seventeen trees. Seventeen trees in Charing Cross Road and nobody sees them.

DS: What about certain images in the Dead Boards series in which a single figure is walking, tentatively advancing one leg in front of the other, in the spaces of those rooms with wooden floors and wooden walls?

GILBERT: Those pieces, I remember very well, are based on a living piece – I don't know if you ever saw that piece – The Red Sculpture. That is very much based on a very slow-motion walk in the world.

GEORGE: The texts from The Red Boxers are very much on that subject.

GILBERT: We used to send out some of these small cards like The Red Boxers and Wooden Air. 'Wooden' was based on that wooden floor. Again it is always based on this isolation, this loneliness.

GEORGE: This is from The Red Sculpture. [Reads] 'In the room we looked across the wooden air between. They moved and paused a little, not seeing anything. Leaning on the windowsill a while, two stonish faces on the floor, and tilted, moved on with dry boards and then to stand. Stillness breathing through our air makes us still breathe.

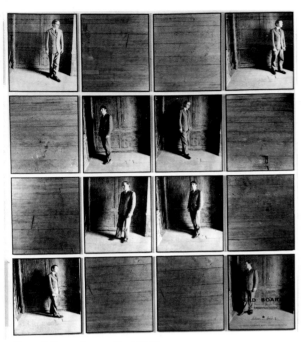

Dead Boards no.7, 1976
247 x 206 cm / 97.25 x 81 ins

Walking across the window glass, dry figures come to them. Back on back, and shooting through the closed study, two in the chapel, with life around the suits.'

Whatever we do, that's it

GILBERT: I think there are two different kinds of artist. We always said we only like the artists who actually deal with human life, not the artists who paint a picture which has nothing to do with the artist. I'm not explaining myself very clearly, George.

GEORGE: Well, there's the artist who does it for himself and the artist who wants to make a happy life, do good pictures and become respected and have a nice holiday house, nice friends, nice meals. Unlike artists who work by ripping from inside themselves and chucking it on the wall and getting damaged in the process. To run the risk of damaging yourself as an artist is the way to get something so truthful that a lady stops you in the street and nearly sobs when she tells you about some piece you've actually forgotten you ever made. Falling into truth. We'll always remember in Baltimore some woman came up and said Black Church Face – the title of one of the pictures – had such an amazing lost look and could have been something to do with a thousand miles away or 30 years ago, but there was an intense connection between her and that picture. A happy artist can't reach that woman.

GILBERT: The artist is it, the artist is the canvas. We are becoming it.

GEORGE: Living sculptures.

GILBERT: We are living sculptures. All the good ones for us are the living monsters, like van Gogh. He became a living sculpture. Don't you think even Rembrandt became a living sculpture, or Francis Bacon became a living sculpture?

GEORGE: The ones who can always speak very clearly from the grave, we think. That's what we'd like to be able to do. If you say William Blake, already I can hear his voice calling, with just the name.

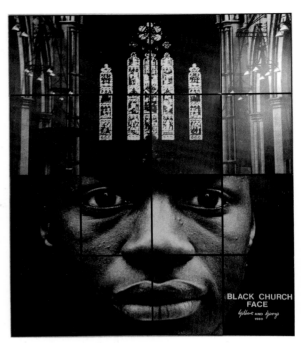

Black Church Face, 1980
241 x 201 cm / 95 x 79 ins

GILBERT: That's why we used to like some of the early Samuel Palmer, when he was totally religious and you feel that every picture is based on spunking religion. That's what we like, not the later work when he learnt about art and was finished for ever. That's why we always want not to know.

GEORGE: We only want to know one thing, and that's that we're wrong. If you're wrong you have a chance. If you're wrong before you actually step into the studio, you're on the right track.

GILBERT: If you know you're wrong, it's fantastic.

GEORGE: From our own research we've figured out that nobody created a great work of art, wrote a great novel, because they knew how to do it. It's only people that don't know how to do it that actually do it.

DS: That's the difference between the artist and the entertainer.

GEORGE: I think that's probably true as well.

DS: The entertainer knows how to get certain effects, and manipulates those effects; the artist works in order to find out how to do it.

GEORGE: So to describe an artist as very polished is the greatest insult obviously.

GILBERT: We would like more and more to liberate ourselves from art.

DS: I believe you never edit when you've done a series.

GEORGE: We would never think of that, we wouldn't even understand that. How would we know? Sometimes a year later we see more clearly what we've done. We would never select from pictures, or from designs for pictures. Not even provisional designs, not even that. If we design 18 pictures or 25 pictures, those are the ones we will make.

DS: But then when you've done a series, you may not be able to show the entire series. In any case, you yourselves will accept every one of them as valid?

GEORGE: Totally, in every single way.

DS: Why?

GEORGE: Because if it comes completely blind, out from inside of ourselves, then it must be true. Every picture is true. It would be very cruel and stupid to start destroying pictures.

GILBERT: It's just like speaking. You say this, then you say that. Double meanings: it's not based on a straight line. Confusion of thought: we love that. Double meanings, that's what we're all about. We accept everything. We accept the flowers and the shit, the totality of everything. Whatever we do, that's it. Who are we to decide what is good and what is bad, when we are making them completely blind, and we trust our feeling, we trust our inner source, totally?

DS: What do you mean when you say that in making them you're completely blind?

GEORGE: We're not conscious, we're never conscious. We have to be completely weird, drugged, zonked, dead-headed. We cannot say 'What pictures are we going to make today?'. What an idiotic idea! What would you do? Trees with monkeys, or... I can't think of anything.

GILBERT: It's very simple. We always try to look inside ourselves. It's not conscious; we let ourselves be driven. We don't know what we will end up with, we don't know anything. We let ourselves be driven, and that's how we do it, and then we accept it.

GEORGE: How would you discriminate between the pictures? It would be impossible at that stage. It would be totally arbitrary. You can't destroy pictures yourself. How would you explain it to the Inland Revenue?

GILBERT: But we do make a selection when we make our drawings. We make a selection then, but it is not a very conscious one, because we have so many images – say, ten to twenty thousand images. We always say that we are like chucking a dart in choosing them. It doesn't matter which ones we choose, because the feelings, the messages are already there. The nervous part of our work is taking things, that's the most difficult part.

DS: Taking the photographs?

GEORGE: Taking the negatives, the actual negatives.

GILBERT: That's the most neurotic part as well, that makes us very neurotic, because once we have that, then it doesn't matter.

DS: And why does it make you neurotic? Because of the intensity of concentration?

GEORGE: Even the responsibility. If we're doing the pictures for people, we have to be accurate.

People want a complicated art

DS: Where do you like your work to be seen, ideally?

GILBERT: I really like it plastered in museums, plastered on the walls like messages.

GEORGE: The profession has yet to realise the enormous hunger for art that is out there.

They're perfectly happy if two or three hundred people come in to their museum in a day. If two per cent of the population attends a museum show they are pleased. We think that's nonsense.

DS: You feel that your work speaks to people who don't normally look at art?

GEORGE: We feel, from our experience of talking to people on the street or wherever, that people want a complicated art. You see, life is unbelievably difficult for a lot of people: family, drugs, money, education, housing; everyone has amazing disasters in their life –

GILBERT: – religiousness, drunkenness –

GEORGE: – Muslimism, Christianity, prison, all this stuff makes an enormously complicated life. In every dear little person on the street there's an enormously complicated life going on. It's difficult, and they can only sort it out a little bit in their dear heads by reading a novel, seeing some pictures. They need something to relate to, to compare with so as to see how they are. They don't want a simple art.

DS: I am very interested in your comparison to the novel. Is there any other art being made at the moment that is comparable to the novel?

GILBERT: Bacon is. He tells a story, or don't you think?

DS: Well, it is interesting that you say that, because he professed to be very much against the telling of a story, but in some of the George Dyer triptychs there is a story, a very strong story.

GILBERT: We don't want a story either, but there is a story. We want a certain existence, that is what we want, a certain complex existence.

GEORGE: The story is the whole life. All the pictures taken together make a story, not one of the pictures. One day there will be a last G & G picture and then you can read the whole story.

GILBERT: We want to create something that is existent, to make something solid, don't you think, George?

GEORGE: Something to connect us with the viewer, with the viewer's life.

GILBERT: That would be a story. I think what changes people, what you call an art that changes people, is subversive, don't you think? It is underneath, it is not a direct telling you what to think, it is all underneath – subversive, subversive. You ask questions, then the viewer starts to ask questions, and at that moment it works.

DS: I take it that you like to show in museums or public galleries not only because the spaces are larger but because ordinary people who would not mind going there are put off by the atmosphere of dealers' galleries in fashionable shopping areas.

GEORGE: It's more difficult for most people to walk into a West End Gallery than to walk into a West End furriers or a West End jeweller's shop. It's very intimidating.

DS: I find it particularly intimidating in New York, myself. I hardly dare to go into any of them.

GEORGE: SoHo is a little different, but Uptown is awkward, yes. Three spotlights on three stupid sculptures and one snotty-nosed girl sitting at the desk looking…

GILBERT: I can't bear the stuck-up girls and I can't bear the typing.

GEORGE: What are they typing, by the way?

GILBERT: Because in some ways we like our art to be completely anarchic, down to earth, brutal, we don't want it to be made to look exclusive. That's what we are against – lighting them up like holy ghosts.

DS: And also putting a lot of space between them?

GEORGE: We are against that because it probably reminds people of a lot of so-called Modern Art which needs that. If you do some damn silly canvas with a black dot in the middle, unless you have it on the wall by itself with two spotlights, nobody would know what the fuck it is. You've got to make it special or it wouldn't be anything anyway. It forces you, like religion makes you wear a hat in church, makes the doors big, heavy doors, has the candles at the end. It forces you to enjoy it. Modern Art had a lot of that in fact, it told everyone they were stupid unless they liked this stuff. We don't think that an artist should use a visual language which eliminates 90 per cent of the population. Because, if you write a book, even on a very complicated, scientific subject, you have to be able to make it explain something. There's no reason why an art-work must be completely baffling to anybody.

GILBERT: It is really interesting that they all talk about modern artists as if modern art were jokes and cynicism.

DS: Can you name an artist today who paints with the kind of earnestness that Bacon did?

GILBERT: I think we are that.

DS: But I think that with you one is never sure where there is irony and where there is not.

GEORGE: I'll tell you where there's irony in our work: nowhere, nowhere, nowhere. Every time we see that word in an article about us we go to the dictionary and I still don't understand the bloody meaning of the word.

GILBERT: And we hate it.

GEORGE: If we do a picture called Urinal, we can't possibly mean that it must be something else, there must be something behind it, it must be ironic. No. We're doing a picture about urinals and all the different complicated thought around that. No member of the general public ever thinks we are ironic, never. That's a professional idea.

GILBERT: I'm convinced that in the moment an art critic takes that away, they will be able to understand us for the first time.

A certain cloud in front of us

DS: When you did The Singing Sculpture you were there in the work – inevitably, as it was a performance piece. When you went on to do the big drawings and paintings of figures in landscapes, you were still there in the work. This time that wasn't inevitable; it was a choice. Did you have any idea then that, so long as you were working together, you were going to choose to put yourselves in virtually all your images?

GEORGE: It didn't really occur to us that we were doing that. Like when you sign a letter you'll never sign another name; it'll always be your name at the end of the letter. We were just in them like that, as far as we were concerned. We were the art.

GILBERT: We do believe that before that we were just experimenting. But then came the moment when we walked out of Fournier Street together and said: 'We are the art'. That was before doing The Singing Sculpture. It was shortly after moving to Fournier Street that we decided we were the object and the subject. And I think that was the biggest invention we ever did. After that, that was it. We made a decision, like another artist who tells himself the most important thing is the form. And for us

the most important thing was us as objects speaking to the world. And we made a decision, and that's why we started all this telephoning, writing letters, doing drawings. We were talking to the world with small letters, small videos, leaving these drawings behind about us, making us the centre of attention. We made ourselves the object. And after that we realised that it was in some way limited. Maybe we could just make ourselves The Singing Sculpture. It was limited what we could actually say to the world. Except dancing. So we discovered this art form that would put ourselves in the pictures, which was limitless.

DS: Is it like artists obsessively doing self-portraits?

GEORGE: We never saw it in terms of self-portraiture really. Not at all. Anyway, for years and years the images we took were of each other, so it wouldn't be a self-portrait anyway.

DS: You always took the pictures of each other?

GEORGE: It took us years to work out. They were always separated and put together artificially.

GILBERT: In some way we are becoming this object that everybody is allowed to look at. Do you understand, David? We became these objects that you are allowed to look at, everybody's allowed to look. We are opening ourselves up, you are allowed to look. We are making ourselves totally visible in all these complicated ways. That's exactly like going to look at a sculpture, no?

DS: Is it anything to do with the way Picasso constantly put himself into his images? He portrays himself as the artist, as the Minotaur, as the cuckold…

GILBERT: But he is the painter, he is the painter painting himself, painting a model, he is the painter laughing at the world. But we are it; we are the objects, we are the naked lady. We ARE the naked lady.

DS: Is there a distinction in your works between those where you are the object and those where you are witnesses? There are certain pictures where you appear as the central figures, but there are a lot of other pictures where you appear rather like images of the donors in Renaissance pictures.

GEORGE: We don't see it as a distinction so much. Even in the pictures where people say, 'You're not in that picture', we don't see it in that way. We are not pictured as artists anyway. We don't have any equipment. You know, the artist usually stands with a bloody brush and palette! We don't have that. We are there like the viewer is there.

DS: Is it linked, your doing this, to the fact that there are two of you?

GEORGE: We couldn't have done The Singing Sculpture as a single person.

GILBERT: I think that's why we are different to other artists – that we made ourselves the object. I think that is the key point.

GEORGE: Every artist always wanted that anyway.

GILBERT: Yes, but they never actually did it, they are still in front of the canvas. We are not in front of the canvas, because we are the canvas. So that's it, that's the big difference.

GEORGE: And with two, self-doubt is removed immediately.

DS: I know that when I install an exhibition – a process which has some slight resemblance to making art – I prefer to work with somebody else, so that we can bounce ideas off each other – to use a phrase I hate.

GEORGE: Not that we do that, but we know what you mean.

DS: But you don't do that?

GILBERT: We don't do that.

GEORGE: That's what we call a collaboration.

DS: And you don't do that. What do you do?

GILBERT: Nothing.

GEORGE: That's the weird thing. People say it must be so exciting, two people working together. It must be so stimulating, this exchange. We don't seem to have had this exchange – it doesn't exist.

DS: It's totally telepathic?

GEORGE: Its partly telepathic, I'm sure. We just have a common ground of experience, of instinct. If we had to bounce ideas off each other there'd be battles! Appaling!

GILBERT: It is always based on a certain cloud in front of us that we are going towards, a certain cloud. It doesn't have to be written down exactly as it is going to be, but so long as we are going towards it, that's it. At that moment it's all very open, only certain things are very important, the rest is totally unimportant. The most important thing is that our art has to be so human, so based on life, that it is not based on art. We made a big decision a long time ago – that we are it, and it with all our failures and everything. With all our complications, that's what's important. We are not it with only being brilliant, we are it with everything, and that is why it works, because we accept it all in that form which is in front of us.

GEORGE: One of our first rules for ourselves was 'Never discuss'. That was in 1970.

The Singing Sculpture, 1970

Spring 1968, St. Martin's School of Art

GILBERT & GEORGE
What Will Survive Of Us Is Love
by
Michael Bracewell

The title of this essay is the last line of a poem called 'An Arundel Tomb', which was written by Philip Larkin in February, 1955, after he saw the six century old monument to the Earl of Arundel and his wife in Chichester Cathedral. The poem describes the way in which the Earl and his wife are shown in effigy lying side by side, holding hands for all eternity, as a testimony to their undying love for one another.

The poem's assured, affirmative conclusion – defiant, in the face of time and change – could double as an apt description of the way in which Gilbert & George, throughout their public epic of self-portraiture, are seen to face the world. Besuited or naked, embracing or holding hands, but always side by side, Gilbert & George are both embodied in their art and the embodiment of their art. Their art is love immortalised as a kind of shrine to mortality itself: the fundamental facts of existence, the reality check.

But there is a secondary sense in which Larkin's poem seems to correspond with the life and work of Gilbert & George, and this relates to a discovery made by Larkin's biographer, Andrew Motion. Concluding his analysis of 'An Arundel Tomb', Motion brings to light a later annotation that was made by Larkin to the poem's manuscript: "Love isn't

stronger than death just because statues hold hands for six hundred years." It's a bleak pronouncement that Larkin has made in this comment, and it seems to be almost wantonly self-punishing in the way it tries to cheat the reader – and more importantly, Larkin himself – of a happy ending.

The smashing of the poem's carefully crafted meditation on life and love, with the single hammer blow of a brutally objective observation, is the action of a cynical realist, or an enraged romantic – which amounts to pretty much the same thing. Faced with the realities of human existence, Larkin's pronouncement on his own work as an artist is neither cocooned in the cosy cotton wool of sentimental religiosity, nor cleverly gift-wrapped with the ribbons and bows of intellectualism and critical theory. On the surface of it, the poet has assumed the manner of the practical man of business, with no time to waste on the elevated fancies of art and fine feelings.

In this much, the temper of Larkin's self-punishing lucidity chimes with an anecdote which George once told to an interviewer, Martin Gayford: "When I first arrived in London, I remember walking down to Limehouse to see the other Hawksmoor church, Saint Anne's – he was the architect of Christ Church at the end of the street where we live. And there was a man standing at the railings looking at the cemetery. I went over to see what he was looking at, and it was Francis Bacon, just gazing into the bloody dead-body yard."

In this little story, George makes no attempt to romanticise either himself as the observer, Bacon as an artist, or the cemetery itself as a place of meditation. Rather, the scene presents itself in the black and white of a monochrome vision: life, death and art – the battleground between reality and romanticism. Or, conversely, the ménage à trois through which those same three factors exist in an addictive, co-dependent, and passionate relationship. For from the very beginning of their extraordinary life together, Gilbert & George seem to have been addressing this fundamental question of how life itself – expressed as the city, more often than not, and more specifically the ancient 'Square Mile' of the City of London – exists between the twin poles of Love and Death.

This is the energising mission which runs throughout their work like a low electrical current, removing them as much from the theories of artistic practice as it does from the safety of an artistic 'school' or 'movement'. (And yet despite this, Gilbert & George make works which fit with great ease into the history of art; after all, they make big, figurative pictures, many of which tell simple stories about the artists and their times. Even the pre-Baroque occupants of the Arundel Tomb wouldn't be that freaked out by the style of these pictures, in terms of their visual language.)

But this questioning of Love and Death would also seem to be the attitude to life which has set Gilbert & George on their endless walk around the City of London. And the meditational walk exists as a kind of tradition within the history of philosophy: think of Socrates' walks around Athens, Rousseau's 'Reveries Of A Solitary Walker', or Kierkegaard's daily circuits of the lakes at Copenhagen. In many of their pictures, Gilbert & George record what they have witnessed on their walks – as colour images – in a way which makes the City streets the map of their souls (you could call it their 'memories' if you're uncomfortable with the word 'souls'), and their innermost selves a map of the City. All they've got is each other – their walks record – and their universe is Fournier Street, in the East-End of London, where they've lived and worked for over thirty years.

With their 'Rudimentary Pictures', Gilbert & George have entered into their fourth decade of working together as one artist. They have become, as a consequence of their very isolation and single-mindedness, an international institution within contemporary culture. Similarly, their significance in popular culture is as extensive as their reputation as visual artists. They destroyed the spurious boundaries between High and Low culture, long before such distinctions were even being recognised. They are probably the only people ever to become great pop stars without having recorded a single tune. And to the common charge that 'their work is hard to look at', they reply that 'it's even harder to create'. Above all, they want their art to be accessible to everyone, because they believe that their pictures are about everyone. But the end comes first: what will survive of them is Love.

ONE: 'Unreal City...' Gilbert & George and The City of London

Like T.S.Eliot's neurasthenic bank clerks, marching to work over London Bridge "with a dead sound on the final stroke of nine", the artists Gilbert & George are essentially modernist extensions of Dickensian characters. Dickens, as the great anatomist-in-prose of London's social body, has set in place a singular perspective on the ancient business district known as the City and its immediate environs. To Dickens, the City and the Chancery, the banks and legal temples, were a mutating force of nature, indifferent to the rise or fall of human expectations and led by the lumpen instinct of greed. The City described by Dickens was the City inherited by Eliot – as both a bank employee and a poet – out of which he fashioned his Waste Land. Hard by there, on the City's eastern fringe, lies Fournier Street, built in 1724 and once housing Huguenot weavers. Here you may now find the artists Gilbert & George.

Back in the middle Sixties, when Gilbert & George first came to Fournier Street, the district was run down and unfrequented. You can get an idea of what their street looked like from the documentary film based on Geoffrey Fletcher's book, 'The London Nobody Knows', which was made in 1967 by Norman Cohen. Even in the Sixties, this was a part of London which would never be swinging. In Cohen's film, our guide around the capital's backwaters is the breathlessly

aristocratic James Mason, dressed in a fine tweed jacket and matching cap, and dropping in on the locals with all of the patrician grace and good manners which was expected in those days of a proper gentleman.

Some clips of this film were used by Gerald Fox in his award-winning films about Gilbert & George for 'The South Bank Show'. You see the drunks on the corner, unsteadily putting down their precious bottles of meths before they take a swing at one another; it's a scene of touching comedy, shot through with tragedy. You get to watch James Mason paying a call on a local woman who now lives in the house where Jack The Ripper stowed one of his victims in the back yard. Far away, thirty two years ago, from the psychedelic, Op-art world of Chelsea, this district which Gilbert & George have defined in their 'Rudimentary Pictures' as 'Fournier World', was like a ghost palace for a disappearing community. Soon, it would become the new home for a succession of ethnic minorities, bringing with them new life and new energy.

Gilbert & George are artists of London in much the same way as Dickens, Eliot or Ford Maddox Ford were writers of London. For them, the City exists as both its real self and as a kind of allegorical world, in which the business of living – the journey between Love and Death – is described in the ceaseless mechanism of the city itself, as a virtually organic form. In Ford Maddox Ford's sadly neglected 'Survey of a Modern City: The Soul of London' – written between 1903 and 1904, when Ford was between bouts of nervous illness – we can find a vision of London which more or less rehearses the London of Gilbert & George.

Throughout their work, Gilbert & George have looked to the streets of East London, its multi-racial mix of teenagers and its haunting, still-life of damage and debris as the mirror of their own journey and the stage of their 'Art For All'. And the complex mapping of the streets of London themselves, reflect the strange maps of human existence which Gilbert & George have identified in the magnified images of their own bodily fluids which they first used in their 'Fundamental' pictures. It is as though these street maps are etched on to the very fundamentals of the human body, like a map of destiny. And with this in mind, it is worth quoting the following passage of Ford Maddox Ford's in full, for it sheds light upon the 'Piss City', 'Blood City', 'Sex City', 'Gum City' and 'Crying City' of the London in the 'Rudimentary Pictures':

"In the country they say that large clocks when they tick solemnly and slowly, thud out the words: 'Alive – Dead; Alive – Dead' – because in this world at every second a child is born, a man dies. But, in London, a listener to the larger clock which ticks off the spirits of successive ages, seems to hear above the roar of the traffic, the slow reverberation: 'Never – Again; Never – Again', as principles rise and die, and rise and die again. For in London that fact forces itself upon the ear and upon the eye; it is a part of the very dust. It is, perhaps, the final lesson of the great, human place. Arts rise and die again, systems rise and die again, faiths are born only to die and

rise once more; the only thing constant and undying is the human crowd."

Having mapped their London as the city of human experience – a place which we can also find in the early political journalism of Dickens, popularly published between 1833 and 1839 as 'Sketches By Boz' – Gilbert & George turn their locality into their universe: the city becomes infinitely transferable, as a thoroughfare of humanity: the great leveller. Their city could be Los Angeles, Moscow, Beijing, Valencia, Naples, or the space-age grid system of Milton Keynes. 'Fournier World', in this respect, becomes universal. Accommodating the forces of lived experience which Eliot described in the Waste Land, and which Dickens saw in the fog which hung from Ludgate Circus to the Essex marshes, the London of Gilbert & George is a wholly real place, "Illustrative" – as the young Dickens wrote – "of Everyday Life, and Everyday People".

TWO: UK 60s, 70s, 80s; punk rock, uber-liberals and ultra-modernists:
A Social Theory of Gilbert & George

Everybody's a teenager – innocent, naive – growing up, getting more religious, getting more sexy. Gilbert

At the ritualised wake for Brian Jones which comprised the free concert given by the Rolling Stones in Hyde Park, on 5th July, 1969, the two most improbably attired

members of the massive crowd must have been Gilbert & George. During their earliest career, Gilbert & George considered the pop form and the pop audience as a possible medium for their work. In an interview which Gilbert & George gave to Anne Seymour in 1971 (and which was subsequently republished by Robert Violette in 'The Words of Gilbert & George', in 1997) they recounted how: "We did a good deal with the Pop world for a short time. We did a different piece for the Marquee Club, but we did 'Underneath the Arches' at the Lyceum Ballroom and at the Plumpton Pop Festival." At The Marquee, George told Gilbert "some rather bloodthirsty stories from comics' and the audience 'liked it'. When The Rolling Stones played in Hyde Park, Gilbert & George's unofficial contribution took the form of their walking through the crowd wearing their multi-coloured metallised heads and hands. Ultimately, however, they 'saw no future' in the pop environment.

It is ironic that Gilbert & George should have abandoned the world of pop. Over the subsequent decades they would be claimed by pop as honourary stars, their methods and example being rediscovered by successive generations. What makes Gilbert & George so significant within the pop format is the very constancy of their image. As dandies and living artworks – what Quentin Crisp described as 'becoming an autofact' – Gilbert & George are Wildean outcasts – perfect pop material; but in one significant sense they short-circuit Oscar Wilde's famous decree from 'The Decay of Lying' : " – it is none the less true that life imitates art far more than art imitates life." And they short that circuit by making the distinction between art and life completely irrelevant.

To this end, imagine the reaction of young people at a Stones concert in 1969, to the presence of two young people of their own age, dressed in sombre business suits but clearly much further out of the ordinary than anyone else in the audience. By dressing as they did – to do what they were doing – Gilbert & George declared themselves to be far more 'modern', liberal and radical than many of their more fashionably dressed peers. In many ways, at The Stones in Hyde Park, three most outrageously dressed people were Mick Jagger in his snow white ballerina's skirt, and Gilbert & George in their suits.

As the French novelist Gustave Flaubert decreed, back in the 1850s, 'You should be regular and natural in your lifestyle, like a bourgeois, so that you may be violent and original in your work.' For Gilbert & George, as honorary pop stars, their besuited appearance and their unwavering residence in London's East End would find a new relevance and a new audience during the brief first wave of punk rock, and punk's immediate impact on the art schools and their students. Even The Marquee and The Lyceum Ballroom would become punk venues; and as archaically cut suits, short hair and black and white images of the inner city gained new fashionability, so

Gilbert & George emerged as having been there all along. And their most important punk statement was the fact that they still didn't want to belong to any movement or school of activity – least of all punk rock.

In their 'Dirty Words' pictures, made in 1977 – coinciding with the radical new aesthetic and generational attitude which was being catalysed by punk, Gilbert & George described an urban scene in which the subversive, the sexual and the deliberately puerile were used as a new language of social disaffection or energising irritant. And even in their title, 'Dirty Words', there was the mordant humour of the punk aesthetic – a humour which simultaneously mocked itself, and its targets.

Gilbert & George frequented or visited most of the punk and New Romantic clubs that sprung up in cramped basements or old nightclubs around London. In the late Seventies and early Eighties, there was a blurring of the boundaries between gay and straight clubs, with the emphasis being on a self-consciously dandyfied stylishness. Importantly, however, Gilbert & George remained as confrontational and extreme – in their matching suits and seemingly choreographed appearance – as they had been back in 1969. They still looked like Eliot's bank clerks, time-travelling through the new London night life of transvestite bars which played minimalist, post-industrial punk music.

In the middle of the Eighties, as the pop climate turned temperate in the emergence of a new, brightly coloured, aspirational form

of pop which kept pace with the Yuppie spree – this, after all, was the period when the City of London itself was suddenly boomed into a designer-conscious wonderland of new buildings, new technology and new services for the newly wealthy – Gilbert & George retained their ambiguity. Their monolithic new triptych – 'Class War', 'Militant', 'Gateway' (1986) and 'Existers' (1984) being prime examples – were both the most accurate portraits of the New Look of the City, but also a continued declaration of outsiderdom and individualism. When they turned up on Jonathan Ross's newly conceived 'youth TV' programme, 'The Last Resort', in the late eighties and did their dance to 'Bend It', their impact was immediate. Like a pair of funny uncles with the seriousness of ghosts.

Throughout their coincidental careers as pop icons, Gilbert & George have maintained their founding theology of 'Art For All' and their 'Laws of The Sculptors'. In some ways, they have shown that individualism derives from a subtle reworking of social conformity. They live Wilde's dictate from 'The Soul of Man Under Socialism' that 'Art is the most intense form of Individualism that the world has known.' In their extreme liberalism – the 'uber-liberalism' which confounds political orthodoxy in an attempt to articulate a personal honesty – Gilbert & George have created an artistic vision which remains eternally modern, eternally confrontational, and unwaveringly concerned with the realities of human existence.

June1999, Gilbert & George, Milton Keynes Gallery

SPELL OF SWEATING	SWEATING	FUCK ALL NAZI'S
CRYING CITY	BLOOD ROADS	KINK
PISS GARDEN	RAIN WHEEL OF LIFE	FLY WALL
BLOOD ATTACK	FLYING SHIT WHEEL OF DEATH	NAKED CEMETERY
SPUNKING	SWEATY SPUNK	GUM CITY
CRYING	EYE WALL	INSIGHT
BLOOD CITY	MONEY SWEAT	MONEY
MONEY CITY	FOURNIER WORLD	IN THEIR ELEMENT
PISS CITY	MARK OWEN SUCKS LEE'S COCK	LOVE SPUNK
CITY SWEAT	CHEJU ISLAND	RAIN ON US
PISS BLOSSOM	IN THE FACE	SEX CITY

SPELL OF SWEATING 1998 226 x 317cm / 89 x 124.75ins

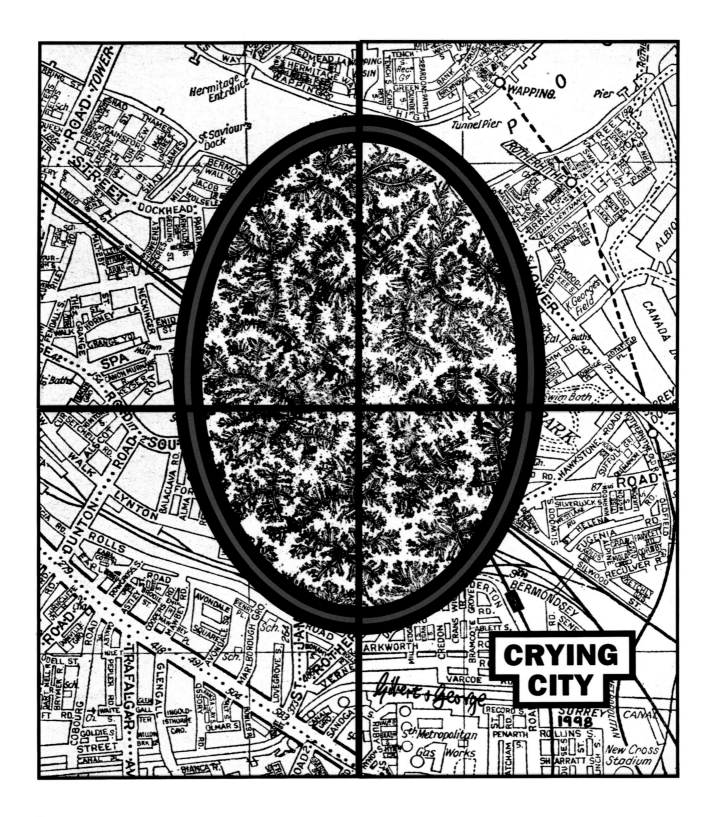

CRYING CITY 1998 151 x 127cm / 59.5 x 50ins

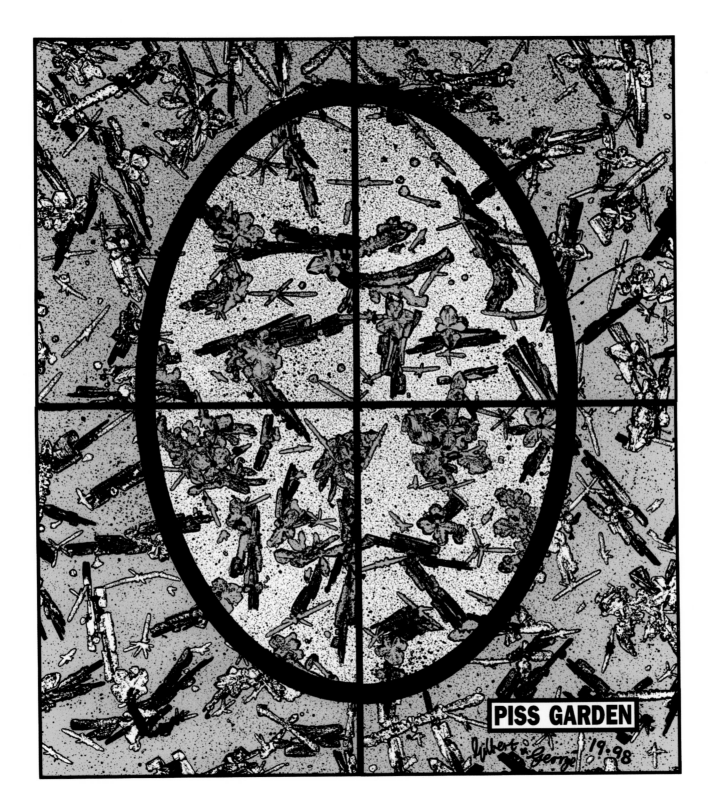

PISS GARDEN 1998 151 x 127cm / 59.5 x 50ins

BLOOD ATTACK

BLOOD ATTACK 1998 127 x 151cm / 50 x 59.5ins

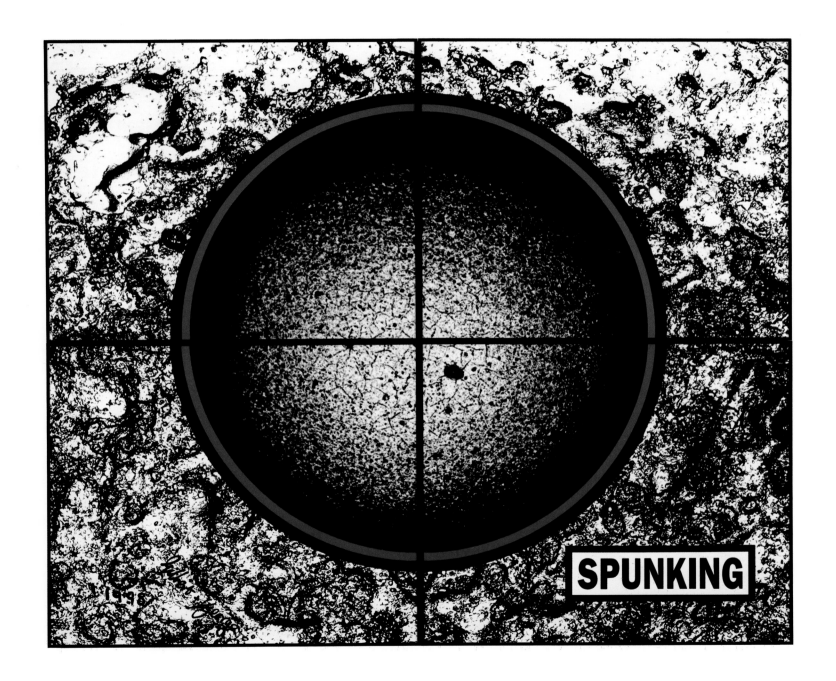

SPUNKING 1998 127 x 151cm / 50 x 59.5ins

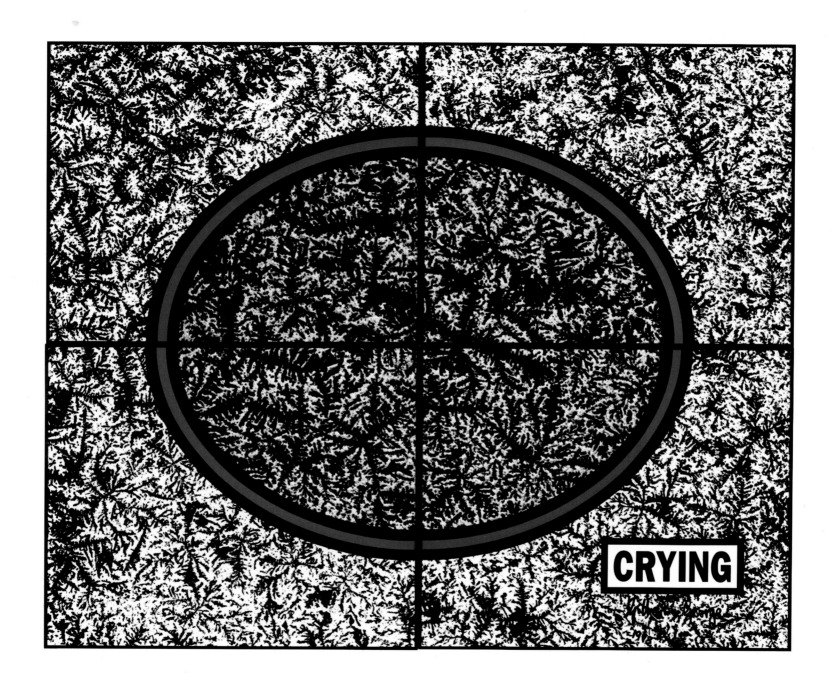

CRYING 1998 127 x 151cm / 50 x 59.5ins

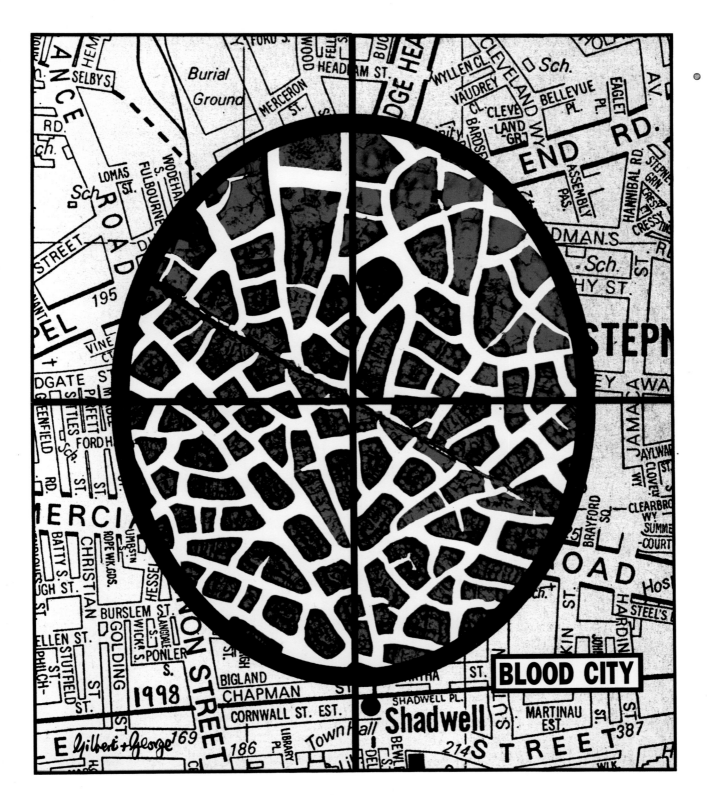

BLOOD CITY 1998 151 x 127cm / 59.5 x 50ins

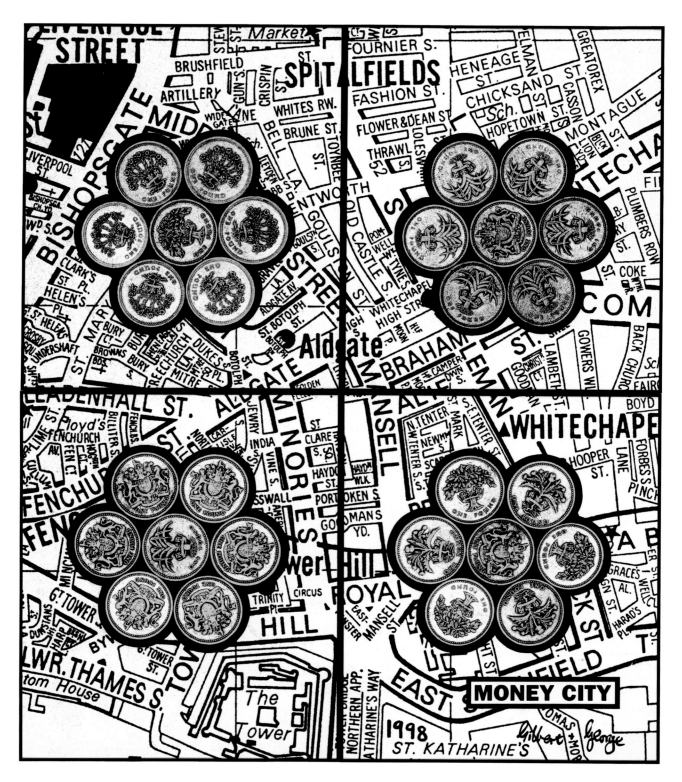

MONEY CITY 1998 151 x 127cm / 59.5 x 50ins

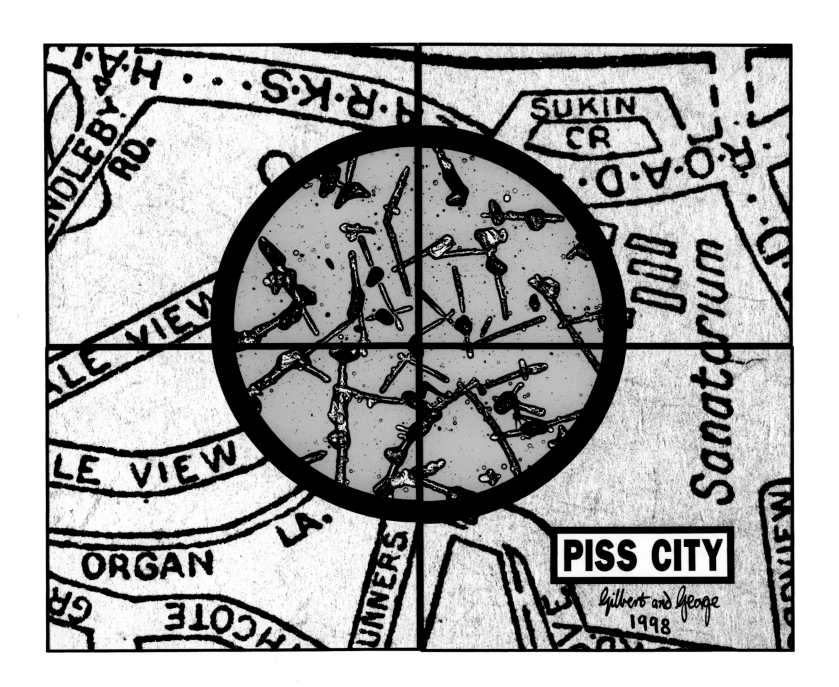

PISS CITY 1998 127 x 151cm / 50 x 59.5ins

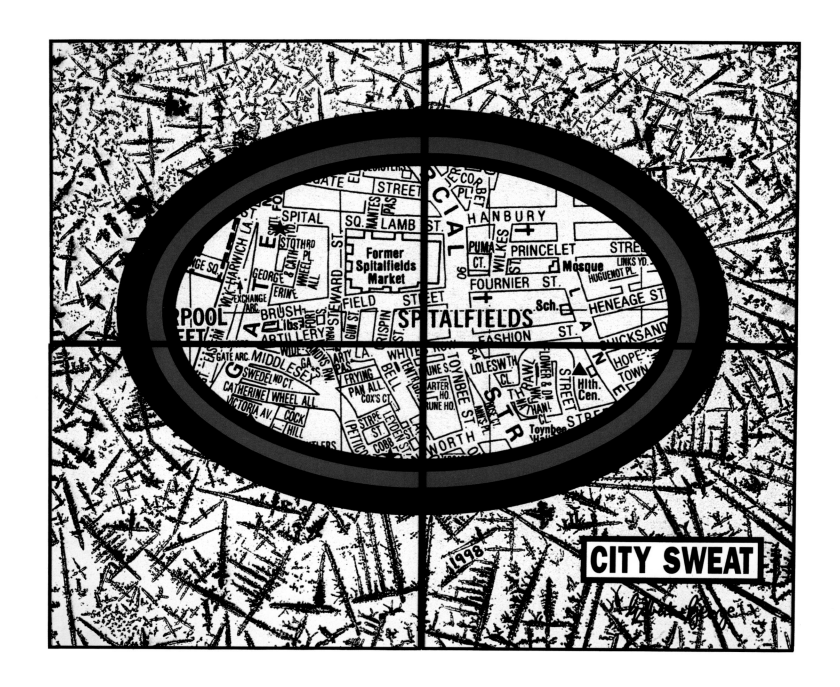

CITY SWEAT 1998 127 x 151cm / 50 x 59.5ins

PISS BLOSSOM 1998 127 x 151cm / 50 x 59.5ins

SWEATING 1998 151 x 127cm / 59.5 x 50ins

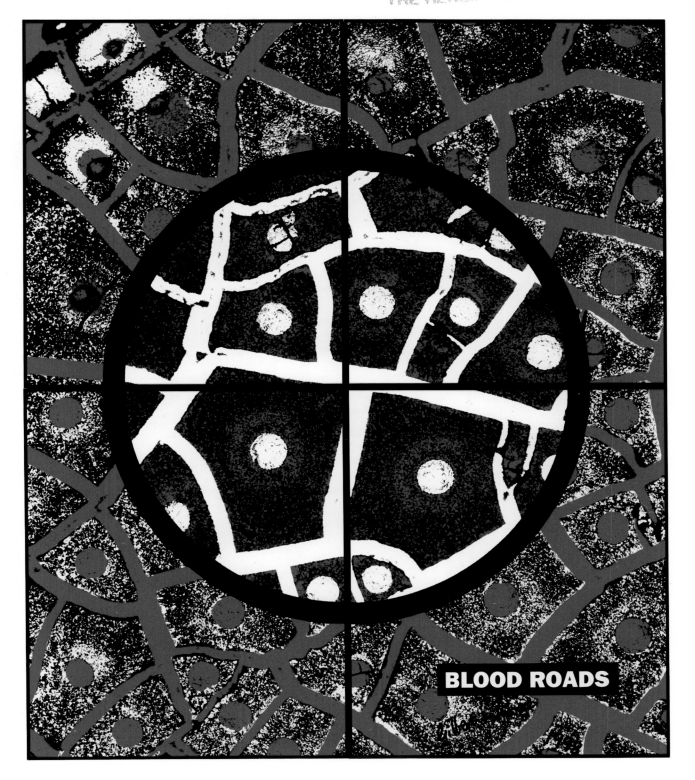

BLOOD ROADS

BLOOD ROADS 1998 151 x 127cm / 59.5 x 50ins

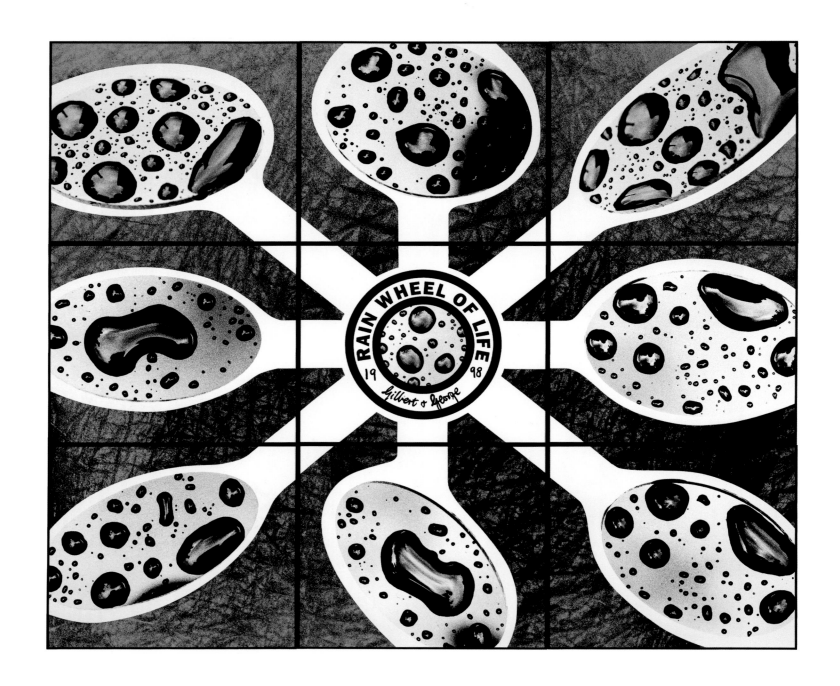

RAIN WHEEL OF LIFE 1998 190 x 226cm / 74.75 x 89ins

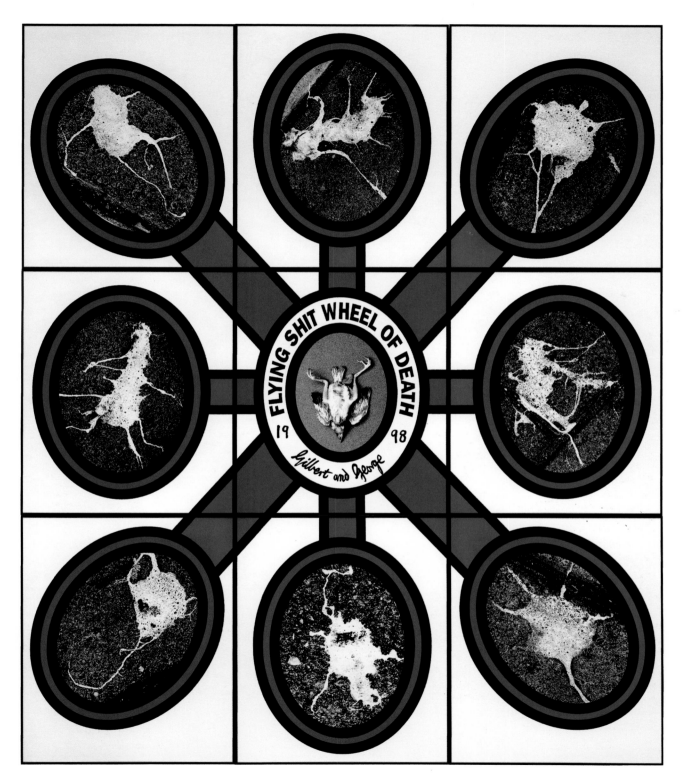

FLYING SHIT WHEEL OF DEATH 1998 226 x 190cm / 89 x 74.75ins

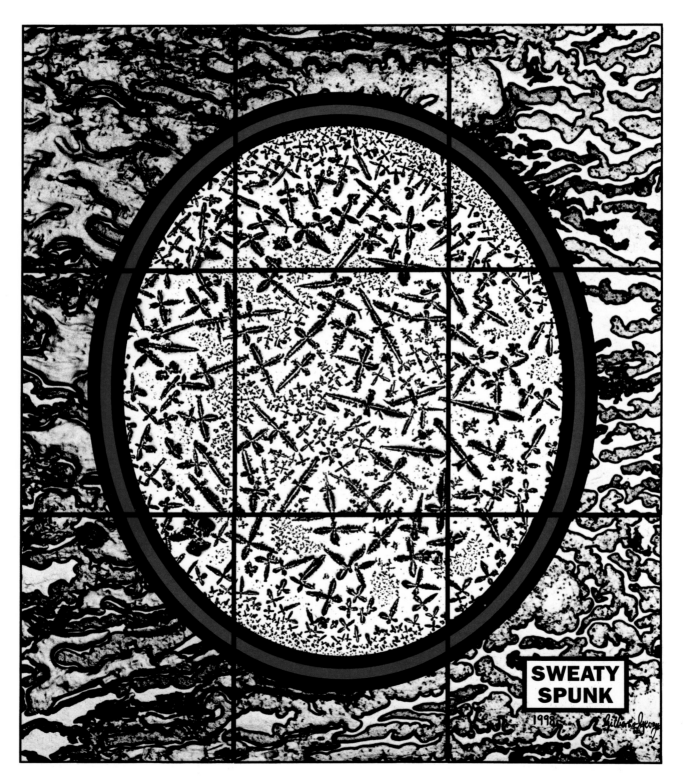

SWEATY SPUNK 1998 226 x 190cm / 89 x 74.75ins

EYE WALL 1998 226 x 190cm / 89 x 74.75ins

MONEY SWEAT 1998 190 x 226cm / 74.75 x 89ins

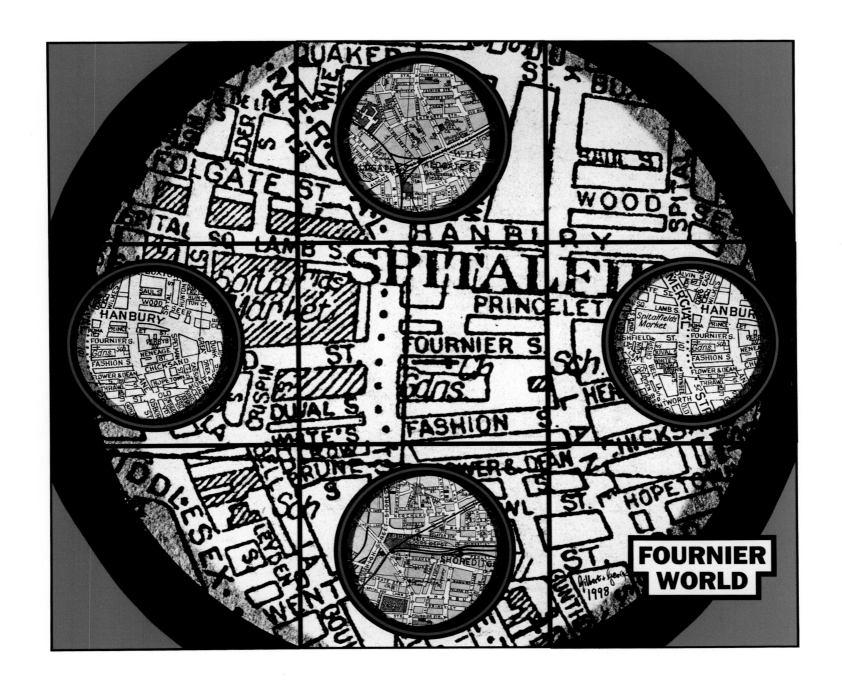

FOURNIER WORLD 1998 190 x 226cm / 74.75 x 89ins

MARK OWEN SUCKS LEE'S COCK 1998 190 x 302cm / 74.75 x 119ins

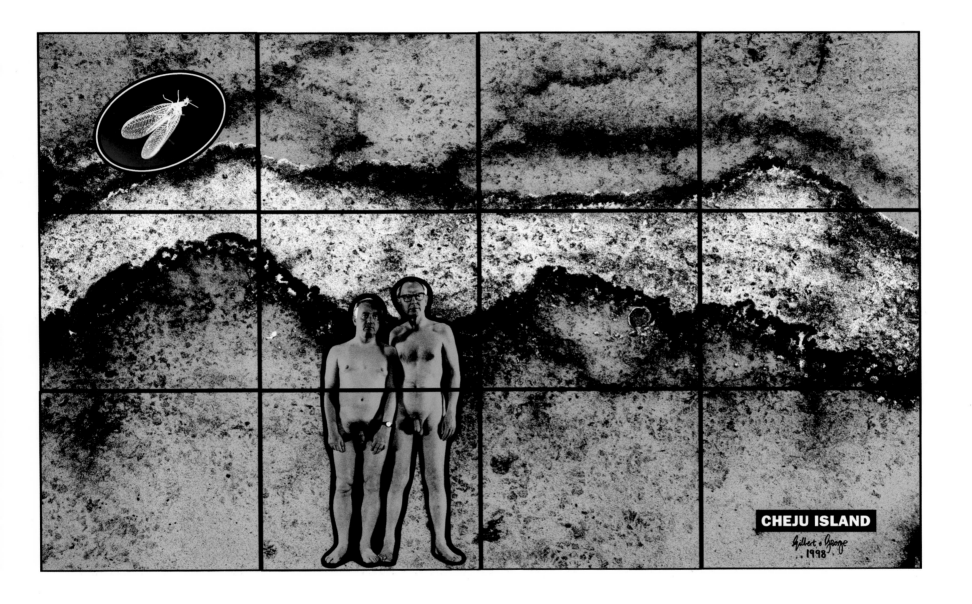

CHEJU ISLAND 1998 190 x 302cm / 74.75 x 119ins

IN THE FACE 1998 190 x 302cm / 74.75 x 119ins

FUCK ALL NAZI'S 1998 190 x 302cm / 74.75 x 119ins

KINK 1998 190 x 377cm / 74.75 x 148.5ins

FLY WALL 1998 190 x 377cm / 74.75 x 148.5ins

NAKED CEMETERY 1998 284 x 338cm / 111.75 x 133ins

GUM CITY 1998 338 x 284cm / 133 x 111.75ins

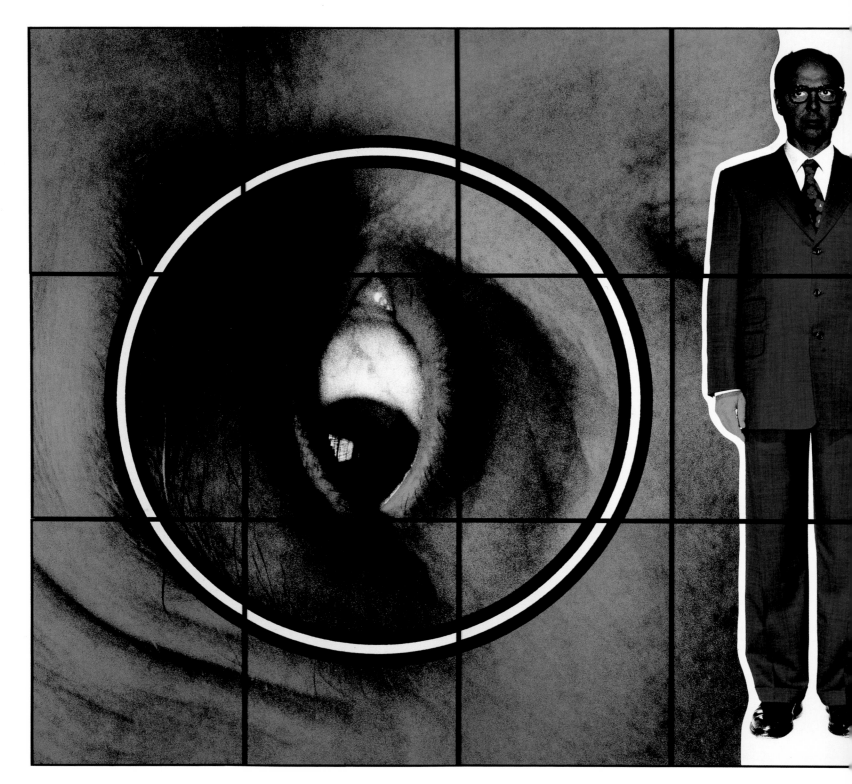

INSIGHT 1998 226 x 508cm / 89 x 200ins

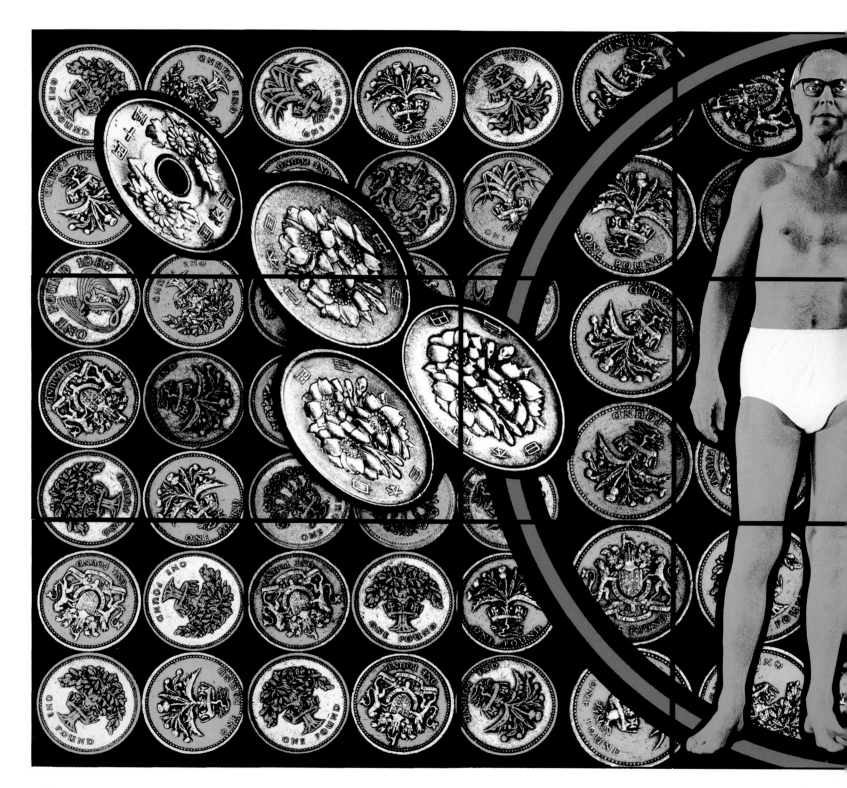

MONEY 1998 226 x 508cm / 89 x 200ins

MONEY

IN THEIR ELEMENT 1998 254 x 528cm / 100 x 207.75ins

LOVE SPUNK 1998 254 x 528cm / 100 x 207.75ins

LOVE SPUNK

Gilbert + George
1998

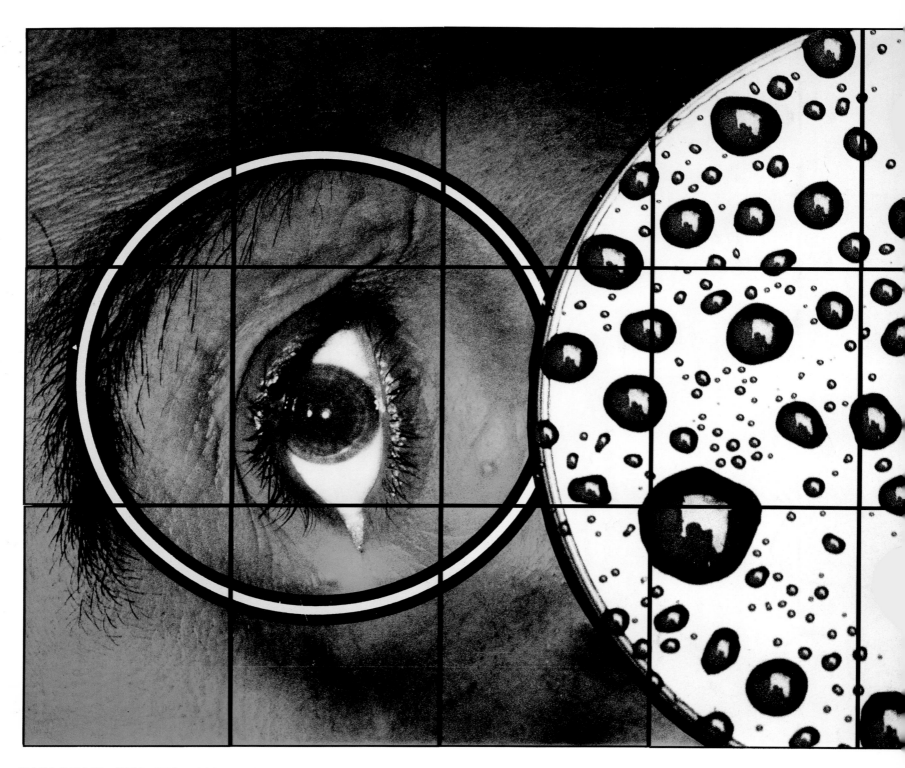

RAIN ON US 1998 253 x 639cm / 99.5 x 251.5ins

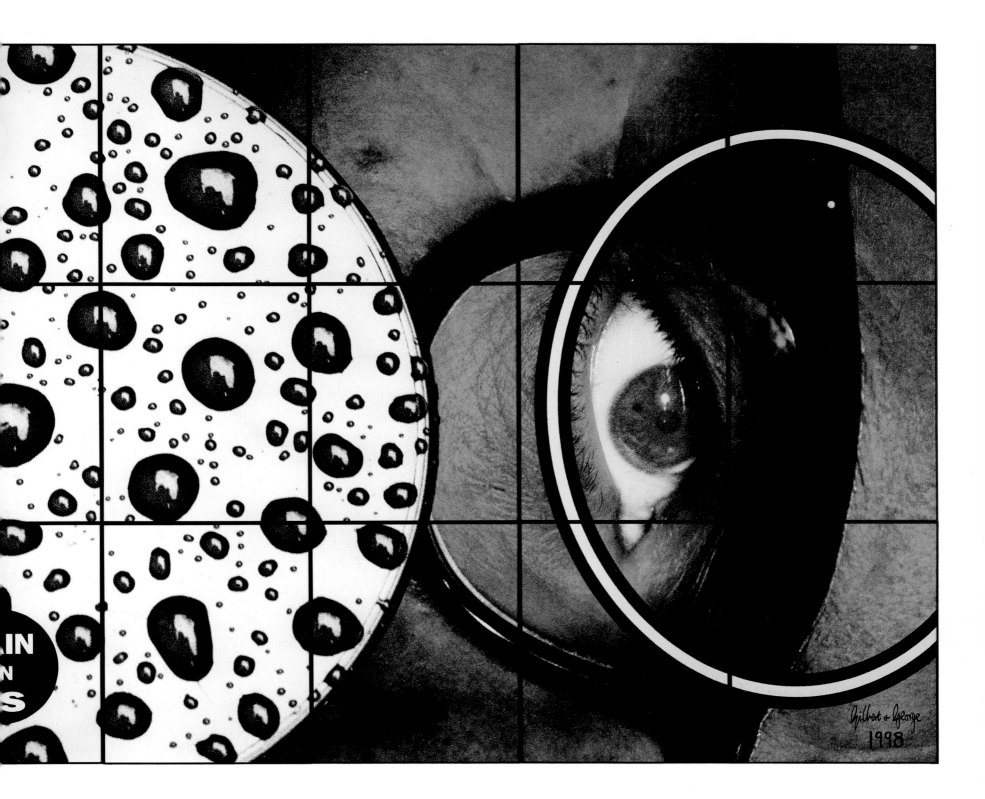

SEX CITY 1998 284 x 591cm / 111.75 x 232.5ins

AFTERWORD
by
Stephen Snoddy

In looking at Gilbert & George's pictures one is immediately struck by the compositional grids that hold the construction of the images. The structure has become a given recognisable signature of their art. In trying to understand anything, order enables the human mind to understand what it is confronted with. Order sorts out the interrelationship of the whole and its parts, as well as the major features from the minor. For instance, charts of mathematical formulae graphically tell us the meaning of the numbers while maps make visible the geographical, economic and social complexion of an area, whether that be in the country or the inner city. A shopping centre is carefully planned out and a co-ordinated display of merchandise in a supermarket helps us in our consumer choice. It is these various orders that permeate throughout life and in Gilbert & George's pictures their grid system is a manifestation, realisation and reflection of an underlying order, be it physical, metaphorical, social or cognitive.

Both Milton Keynes and Gilbert & George use planning as an exercise that requires careful preparation, analysis and prediction. The planning of how to develop Milton Keynes or for Gilbert & George to make new pictures has to at a certain point, give way to making decisions. This considered process can be clear, obscure or even mystical, as Calvino suggests in 'Invisible Cities'.

'What meaning does your construction have?' he asks... 'Where is the plan you are following, the blueprint?'

'We will show it to you as soon as the working day is over; we cannot interrupt our work now,' they answer.

Work stops at sunset. Darkness falls over the building site. The sky is filled with stars. 'There is the blueprint,' they say.

Milton Keynes is the antithesis of an English city. It is the product of clear thought, of planning; a most un-British activity, as cities in the British mind grow organically, from the heart and not from the mind. Milton Keynes is not a quaint, history lesson, it is not for the romantic who dwells upon the past but for the rational who admires its rigorous logic and its order. The original layout, later to be castigated by some as a little Los Angeles, was formed and adapted to the lie of the land. Milton Keynes is like Gilbert & George, bold, new, universal, contentious, progressive and democratic. The orderly grids of Gilbert & George are perfectly in tune with the look of Milton Keynes, and interestingly there happens to be a symbiotic relationship between the short history and life and times of Milton Keynes and the careers of Gilbert & George. The original blueprint and concept of Milton Keynes, drawn up in 1967, (the same year Gilbert & George met at St. Martin's School of Art) was to give an opportunity for the overspill of the East-End of London to move out of London for a fresh start, a new beginning. Many have stayed, many have had children and they have stayed; the first generation is becoming the second generation and the second generation is thinking about a third generation. Milton Keynes and Gilbert & George are iconoclastic and nihilistic for positive gain and the people of Milton Keynes are to the city what Gilbert & George are to each other. A bond that symbolises and personifies a pioneer spirit, as rebels with causes and as outsiders to the norm.

The order of Milton Keynes and Gilbert & George reflect a genuine, sought for, true, original and profound view of life. While Milton Keynes at the end of the 20th century strives for utopian ideals and Gilbert & George work towards definitive statements in their pictures, the new millennium fast approaches but this only marks a moment. The stream of life will continue.

July 1999, aerial photograph of Central Milton Keynes

GILBERT & GEORGE

GILBERT	**GEORGE**
Born Dolomites, Italy 1943	Born Devon, England 1942
Studied	**Studied**
Wolkenstein School of Art	Dartington Adult Education
Hallein School of Art Centre	Dartington Hall College of Art
Munich Academy of Art	Oxford School of Art

Met and studied

St. Martin's School of Art, 1967

GALLERY EXHIBITIONS

1968

THREE WORKS/THREE WORKS	Frank's Sandwich Bar, London
SNOW SHOW	St. Martin's School of Art, London
BACON 32	Allied Services, London
CHRISTMAS SHOW	Robert Fraser Gallery, London

1969

ANNIVERSARY	Frank's Sandwich Bar, London
SHIT AND CUNT	Robert Fraser Gallery, London

1970

GEORGE BY GILBERT & GILBERT BY GEORGE	Fournier Street, London
THE PENCIL ON PAPER DESCRIPTIVE WORKS	Konrad Fischer Gallery, Dusseldorf
ART NOTES AND THOUGHTS	Art & Project, Amsterdam
FROZEN INTO THE NATURE FOR YOU ART	Françoise Lambert Gallery, Milan
THE PENCIL ON PAPER DESCRIPTIVE WORKS	Skulima Gallery, Berlin
FROZEN INTO THE NATURE FOR YOU ART	Heiner Friedrich Gallery, Cologne
TO BE WITH ART IS ALL WE ASK	Nigel Greenwood Gallery, London

1971

THERE WERE TWO YOUNG MEN	Sperone Gallery, Turin
THE GENERAL JUNGLE	Sonnabend Gallery, New York
THE TEN SPEECHES	Nigel Greenwood Gallery, London
NEW PHOTO-PIECES	Art & Project, Amsterdam

1972

NEW PHOTO-PIECES	Konrad Fischer Gallery, Dusseldorf
THREE SCULPTURES ON VIDEO TAPE	Gerry Schum Video Gallery, Dusseldorf
THE BAR	Anthony d'Offay Gallery, London
THE EVENING BEFORE THE MORNING AFTER	Nigel Greenwood Gallery, London
IT TAKES A BOY TO UNDERSTAND A BOY'S POINT OF VIEW	Situation Gallery, London
NEW SCULPTURE	Sperone Gallery, Rome

1973

ANY PORT IN A STORM	Sonnabend Gallery, Paris
RECLINING DRUNK	Nigel Greenwood Gallery, London
MODERN RUBBISH	Sonnabend Gallery, New York
NEW DECORATIVE WORKS	Sperone Gallery, Turin

1974

DRINKING SCULPTURES	Art & Project/MTL Gallery, Antwerp
HUMAN BONDAGE	Konrad Fischer Gallery, Dusseldorf
DARK SHADOW	Art & Project, Amsterdam
DARK SHADOW	Nigel Greenwood Gallery, London
CHERRY BLOSSOM	Sperone Gallery, Rome

1975

BLOODY LIFE	Sonnabend Gallery, Paris
BLOODY LIFE	Sonnabend Gallery, Geneva
BLOODY LIFE	Lucio Amelio Gallery, Naples
POST-CARD SCULPTURES	Sperone Westwater Fischer, New York
BAD THOUGHTS	Gallery Spillemaekers, Brussels
DUSTY CORNERS	Art Agency, Tokyo

1976		
DEAD BOARDS	Sonnabend Gallery, New York	
MENTAL	Robert Self Gallery, London	
MENTAL	Robert Self Gallery, Newcastle	
RED MORNING	Sperone Fischer Gallery, Basel	
1977		
DIRTY WORDS PICTURES	Art & Project, Amsterdam	
DIRTY WORDS PICTURES	Konrad Fischer Gallery, Dusseldorf	
1978		
PHOTO-PIECES	Dartington Hall Gallery, Dartington Hall	
NEW PHOTO-PIECES	Sonnabend Gallery, New York	
NEW PHOTO-PIECES	Art Agency, Tokyo	
1980		
POST-CARD SCULPTURES	Art & Project, Amsterdam	
POST-CARD SCULPTURES	Konrad Fischer Gallery, Dusseldorf	
NEW PHOTO-PIECES	Karen & Jean Bernier Gallery, Athens	
NEW PHOTO-PIECES	Sonnabend Gallery, New York	
MODERN FEARS	Anthony d'Offay Gallery, London	
PHOTO-PIECES 1980-1981	Chantel Crousel Gallery, Paris	
1982		
CRUSADE	Anthony d'Offay Gallery, London	
1983		
MODERN FAITH	Sonnabend Gallery, New York	
PHOTO-PIECES 1980-1982	David Bellman Gallery, Toronto	
NEW WORKS	Crousel-Hussenot Gallery, Paris	
1984		
THE BELIEVING WORLD	Anthony d'Offay Gallery, London	
HANDS UP	Gallery Schellmann & Kluser, Munich	
LIVES	Gallery Pieroni, Rome	
1985		
NEW MORAL WORKS	Sonnabend Gallery, New York	

1987	
NEW PICTURES	Anthony d'Offay Gallery, London
NEW PICTURES	Sonnabend Gallery, New York
1988	
THE 1988 PICTURES	Ascan Crone Gallery, Hamburg
THE 1988 PICTURES	Sonnabend Gallery, New York
1989	
THE 1988 PICTURES	Christian Stein Gallery, Milan
FOR AIDS EXHIBITION	Anthony d'Offay Gallery, London
1990	
GILBERT & GEORGE	Hirschl and Adler Modern, New York
25 WORLDS BY GILBERT & GEORGE	Robert Miller Gallery, New York
THE COSMOLOGICAL PICTURES	Sonnabend Gallery, New York
WORLDS & WINDOWS	Anthony d'Offay Gallery, London
ELEVEN WORLDS BY GILBERT & GEORGE AND ANTIQUE CLOCKS	Desire Feurele Gallery, Cologne
1991	
20TH ANNIVERSARY EXHIBITION	Sonnabend Gallery, New York
1992	
NEW DEMOCRATIC PICTURES	Anthony d'Offay Gallery, London
1994	
GILBERT & GEORGE	Robert Miller Gallery, New York
THE NAKED SHIT PICTURES	Galerie Rafael Jablonka, Cologne
1995	
GILBERT & GEORGE	Galerie Nikolas Sonne, Berlin
1997	
THE FUNDAMENTAL PICTURES	Sonnabend Gallery/Lehmann Maupin, New York

1998

SELECTED WORKS FROM THE FUNDAMENTAL PICTURES	Massimo Martino Fine Arts & Projects, Switzerland
NEW TESTAMENTAL PICTURES	Galerie Thaddaeus Ropac, Paris
NEW TESTAMENTAL PICTURES	Galerie Thaddaeus Ropac, Salzburg
BLACK WHITE AND RED 1971 TO 1980	James Cohan Gallery, New York

2000

| THE RUDIMENTARY PICTURES | Gagosian Gallery, Los Angeles |

MUSEUM EXHIBITIONS

1971

THE PAINTINGS	Whitechapel Art Gallery, London
THE PAINTINGS	Stedelijk Museum, Amsterdam
THE PAINTINGS	Kunstverein, Dusseldorf

1972

| THE PAINTINGS | Koninklijk Museum voor Schone Kunsten, Antwerp |

1973

| THE SHRUBBERIES & SINGING SCULPTURE | National Gallery of New South Wales, Sydney (a John Kaldor Project) |
| THE SHRUBBERIES & SINGING SCULPTURE | National Gallery of Victoria, Melbourne (a John Kaldor Project) |

1976

| THE GENERAL JUNGLE | Albright-Knox Gallery, Buffalo |

1980

| PHOTO-PIECES 1971-1980 | Stedelijk van Abbemuseum, Eindhoven |

1981

PHOTO-PIECES 1971-1980	Kunsthalle, Dusseldorf
PHOTO-PIECES 1971-1980	Kunsthalle, Bern
PHOTO-PIECES 1971-1980	Georges Pompidou Centre, Paris
PHOTO-PIECES 1971-1980	Whitechapel Art Gallery, London

1984

GILBERT & GEORGE	The Baltimore Museum of Art, Baltimore
GILBERT & GEORGE	Contemporary Arts Museum, Houston
GILBERT & GEORGE	The Norton Gallery of Art, West Palm Beach, Florida

1985

| GILBERT & GEORGE | Milwaukee Art Museum, Milwaukee |
| GILBERT & GEORGE | The Solomon R Guggenheim Museum, New York |

1986

PICTURES 1982 TO 85	CAPC, Bordeaux
CHARCOAL ON PAPER SCULPTURES 1970 TO 1974	CAPC, Bordeaux
THE PAINTINGS 1971	The Fruitmarket Gallery, Edinburgh
PICTURES 1982 TO 85	Kunsthalle, Basel
PICTURES 1982 TO 85	Palais des Beaux Arts, Brussels

1987

PICTURES 1982 TO 85	Palacio de Velazquez, Madrid
PICTURES 1982 TO 85	Lenbachaus, Munich
PICTURES 1982 TO 85	Hayward Gallery, London
PICTURES	Aldrich Museum, Connecticut

1990

| PICTURES 1983-88 | Central House of the Artists, New Tretyakov Gallery, Moscow |

1991

| THE COSMOLOGICAL PICTURES | Palac Sztuki, Krakow |
| THE COSMOLOGICAL PICTURES | Palazzo delle Esposizioni, Rome |

1992

THE COSMOLOGICAL PICTURES	Kunsthalle, Zürich
THE COSMOLOGICAL PICTURES	Wiener Secession, Vienna
THE COSMOLOGICAL PICTURES	Ernst Múzeum, Budapest
THE COSMOLOGICAL PICTURES	Haags Gemeentemuseum, The Hague
NEW DEMOCRATIC PICTURES	Aarhus Kunstmuseum, Aarhus
THE COSMOLOGICAL PICTURES	Irish Museum of Modern Art, Dublin

THE COSMOLOGICAL PICTURES	Fundació Joan Miró, Barcelona

1993

THE COSMOLOGICAL PICTURES	Tate Gallery Liverpool
THE COSMOLOGICAL PICTURES	Württembergischer Kunstverein, Stuttgart
GILBERT & GEORGE CHINA EXHIBITION	National Art Gallery, Beijing
GILBERT & GEORGE CHINA EXHIBITION	The Art Museum, Shanghai

1994

GILBERT & GEORGE	Museo d'Atre Moderna della Citta di Lugano, Lugano
SHITTY NAKED HUMAN WORLD	Wolfsburg Kunstmuseum, Germany

1995

THE NAKED SHIT PICTURES	South London Art Gallery, London

1996

THE NAKED SHIT PICTURES	Stedelijk Museum, Amsterdam
GILBERT & GEORGE RETROSPECTIVE	Galleria d'Arte Moderna, Bologna

1997

GILBERT & GEORGE RETROSPECTIVE	Sezon Museum, Tokyo
GILBERT & GEORGE	Magasin 3, Stockholm
GILBERT & GEORGE RETROSPECTIVE	Musée d'Art Moderne de la Ville, Paris

1998

NEW TESTAMENTAL PICTURES	Museo di Capodimonte, Naples

1999

GILBERT & GEORGE 1970-1988	Astrup Fearnley Museet for Moderne Kunst, Oslo
GILBERT & GEORGE 1986-1997	Drassanes, València
THE RUDIMENTARY PICTURES	Milton Keynes Gallery, Milton Keynes (inaugural exhibition)

GILBERT & GEORGE 1991-1997	Ormeau Baths Gallery, Belfast

GROUP EXHIBITIONS (selected)

1969

CONCEPTION	Stadtisches Museum, Leverkusen

1970

INFORMATION	The Museum of Modern Art, New York
18 PARIS IV 66	Rue Mouffetard, Paris
CONCEPTUAL ART, ARTE POVERA, LAND ART	Civic Gallery of Modern Art, Turin
(UNTITLED)	C.A.Y.C., Buenos Aires
PLANS AND PROJECTS	Kunsthalle, Bern

1971

PROSPECT 71 PROJECTION	Kunsthalle, Dusseldorf
THE BRITISH AVANT-GARDE	Cultural Center, New York
SITUATION/CONCEPT	Innsbruck

1972

DOCUMENTA 5	Kassel
THE NEW ART	Hayward Gallery, London
CONCEPT KUNST	Kunstmuseum, Basel

1973

CRITICS CHOICE	Tooth Gallery, London
ART AS PHOTOGRAPHY	Kunstverein, Hannover and touring
FROM HENRY MOORE TO GILBERT AND GEORGE	Palais des Beaux Arts, Brussels
11 ENGLISH DRAWERS	Kunsthalle, Baden-Baden
11 ENGLISH DRAWERS	Kunsthalle, Bremen
CONTEMPORANEA	Villa Borghese, Rome

1974

WORD WORKS	Mt. San Antonio College, California
MEDIUM PHOTOGRAPHY	Kunstverein, Hamburg and touring
KUNST BLEIBT KUNST	Kunsthalle, Cologne
PROSPECT	Kunsthalle, Dusseldorf

1976

ARTE INGLESE OGGI — Palazzo Reale, Milan

THE ARTIST AND
THE PHOTOGRAPH — Israel Museum, Jerusalem

1977

EUROPE IN THE 70's — Art Institute of Chicago and touring into 1979

1978

MADE BY SCULPTORS — Stedelijk Museum, Amsterdam

DOCUMENTA 6 — Kassel

38TH VENICE BIENNALE — Venice

WORKS FROM THE
CREX COLLECTION — Louisiana Museum, Humelbaek and touring

1979

ON WALKS AND TRAVELS — Bonnefantenmuseum, Maastricht

UN CERTAIN ART ANGLAIS — Musée d'Art Moderne de la Ville, Paris

WAHRENHMUNGEN,
AUFZEICHUNGEN, MITTEILUNG — Museum Haus Lange, Krefeld

HAYWARD ANNUAL — Hayward Gallery, London

GERRY SCHUM — Stedelijk Museum, Amsterdam and touring

1980

KUNST IN EUROPE NA '68 — Museum voor Hedendaagse Kunst, Ghent

1981

EXPLORATIONS IN THE 70's — Plan For Art, Pittsburgh

ARTIST AND CAMERA — Arts Council of GB, touring

1981

WESTKUNST — Cologne

16 BIENAL DE SÃO PAULO — São Paulo

BRITISH SCULPTURE IN
THE TWENTIETH CENTURY — Whitechapel Art Gallery, London

PROJECT 6: ART INTO THE 80's — Walker Art Gallery, Liverpool

1982

ATTITUDES, CONCEPTS,
IMAGES 60/80 — Stedelijk Museum, Amsterdam

ASPECTS OF BRITISH ART TODAY — Metropolitan Art Museum, Tokyo

DOCUMENTA 7 — Kassel

ZEITGEIST — Martin Gropius Bau, Berlin

1983

PHOTOGRAPHY IN
CONTEMPORARY ART — National Museum of Modern Art, Tokyo

NEW ART — Tate Gallery London

URBAN PULSERS:
THE ARTIST AND THE CITY — Plan for Art, Pittsburgh

1984

THE CRITICAL EYE — Yale Center for British Art, New Haven

ARTISTIC COLLABORATION
IN THE 20TH CENTURY — Hirshhorn Museum and Sculpture Garden, Washington, D.C.

HISTOIRES DE SCULPTURE — Chateau Des Ducs D'Eperon, Cadillac-Gironde and touring

COLLECTIE BECHT — Stedelijk Museum, Amsterdam

ROSC — The Guinness Hop Store, Dublin

CONTENT — Hirshhorn Museum and Sculpturre Garden, Washington, D.C.

VIA NEW YORK — Musée d'Art Contemporain, Montreal

GILBERT & GEORGE/
RICHARD LONG — Museum of Art, North Carolina

PHOTOGRAPHY IN
CONTEMPORARY ART — The National Museum of Art, Tokyo and Kyoto

COLLECTION ANNICK
AND ANTON HERBERT — Van Abbemuseum, Eindhoven

PRIVATE SYMBOL:
SOCIAL METAPHOR
5TH SYDNEY BIENNALE — Art Gallery of New South Wales, Sydney

THE BRITISH SHOW — Art Gallery of Western Australia, Perth and touring

THE BRITISH ART SHOW 3 — Arts Council of GB, touring

TURNER PRIZE EXHIBITION — Tate Gallery London

DIALOG — The Moderna Museet, Stockholm

1985
OVERTURE — Castello di Rivoli, Torino
PARIS BIENNALE — Grande Halle, La Villette, Paris
CARNEGIE INTERNATIONAL — Carnegie Institute, Pittsburgh
ONE CITY A PATRON — Scottish Arts Council, Edinburgh and touring
A JOURNEY THROUGH CONTEMPORARY ART — Hayward Gallery, London

1986
MATER DULCISSIMA — Chiesa Dei Cavalieri Di Malta, Siracusa
FORTY YEARS OF MODERN ART — Tate Gallery London
FALLS THE SHADOW — Hayward Gallery, London

1987
BRITISH ART IN THE 20TH CENTURY — Royal Academy of Arts, London
CURRENT AFFAIRS — Museum of Modern Art, Oxford and tour to Budapest, Prague and Warsaw

1988
RED YELLOW BLUE – THE PRIMARY COLOURS IN 20TH CENTURY ART — Kunstmuseum, St. Gallen
COLLECTION SONNABEND — Reina Sofia, Madrid

1989
BILDERSTREIT — Kolner Messe, Cologne

1990
THE GREAT BRITISH ART SHOW — McLennan Galleries, Glasgow

1991
METROPOLIS — Martin Gropius Bau, Berlin

1992
POUR LA SUITE DU MONDE — Musée d'Art Contemporain de Montreal
ALL ROADS LEAD TO ROME — Palazzo delle Exposiionzi, Rome

1994
COUPLETS — Stedelijk Museum, Amsterdam

24 — Anthony d'Offay Gallery, London
VISIONS URBAINES — Georges Pompidou Centre, Paris
INAUGURAL EXHIBITION — Wolfsburg Kunstmuseum, Germany
SCULPTURE — Anthony d'Offay Gallery, London

1995
ATTITUDES/SCULPTURES — CAPC, Bordeaux

1996
LA VIE MODERNE EN EUROPE 1870-1996 — Museum of Contemporary Art, Tokyo

1997
TREASURE ISLAND — Fundação Calouste Gulbenkian, Lisbon
DAS ZWANZIGSTE JAHRHUNDERT — Zeitgeist-Gesellschaft, Berlin
THE 2ND KWANGJU BIENNALE — Korea

1998
ART TREASURES OF ENGLAND — Royal Academy of Arts, London

PUBLICATIONS

1970
THE PENCIL ON PAPER DESCRIPTIVE WORKS (edition 500) — Publ. by Gilbert & George, London
ART NOTES AND THOUGHTS — Publ. by Gilbert & George, London
TO BE WITH ART IS ALL WE ASK (edition 300) — Publ. by Gilbert & George, London
A GUIDE TO THE SINGING SCULPTURE — Publ. by Gilbert & George, London

1971
THE PAINTINGS — Publ. by Kunstverein, Dusseldorf
SIDE BY SIDE (edition 600) — Publ. by Konig Bros., Cologne
A DAY IN THE LIFE OF GILBERT & GEORGE (edition 1,000) — Publ. by Gilbert & George, London

1972

'OH, THE GRAND OLD
DUKE OF YORK'

Publ. by Kunstmuseum, Lucerne

1973

CATALOGUE FOR
GILBERT & GEORGE
AUSTRALIAN VISIT

Publ. by John Kaldor, Sydney

1976

DARK SHADOW (edition 2,000)

Publ. by Nigel Greenwood, London

1977

GILBERT & GEORGE

Publ. by Taxispalais Gallery, Innsbruck

1980

GILBERT & GEORGE 1968 TO 1980

Intro. by Carter Ratcliffe,
Publ. by Van Abbemuseum, Eindhoven

1984

GILBERT & GEORGE

Intro. by Brenda Richardson,
Publ. by The Baltimore Museum of Art

1985

DEATH HOPE LIFE FEAR

Intro. by Rudi Fuchs,
Publ. by Castello di Rivoli,Torino

1986

THE CHARCOAL ON PAPER
SCULPTURES 1970-1974

Intro. by Demosthenes Davvatas,
Publ. by CAPC, Bordeaux

THE PAINTINGS 1971

Intro. by Wolf Jahn, Publ. by The
Fruitmarket Gallery, Edinburgh

THE COMPLETE PICTURES
1971–1985

Text by Carter Ratcliff,
Publ. by Thames & Hudson

1989

FOR AIDS EXHIBITION

Introduction by Gilbert & George,
Publ. by Anthony d'Offay Gallery,
London

THE ART OF
GILBERT & GEORGE

by Wolf Jahn,
Publ. by Thames & Hudson, London

1990

THE MOSCOW CATALOGUE

Texts in Russian by Sergei Klokov and
Brenda Richardson
Publ. by Gilbert & George and
Anthony d'Offay Gallery, London

25 WORLDS AND WINDOWS

Text by Robert Rosenblum, Publ. by
Robert Miller Gallery, New York

WORLDS AND WINDOWS

Text by Robert Rosenblum, Publ. by
Anthony d'Offay Gallery, London /
Robert Miller Gallery, New York

ELEVEN WORLDS

by Gilbert & George and Antique Clocks,
Introduction by Remo Guidieri,
Publ. by Desire Feurele, Cologne

GILBERT & GEORGE: POSTCARD
SCULPTURES AND EPHEMERA
1969-1981

Introduction by Carter Ratcliff,
Publ. by Hirschl and Adler, New York

1991

MONARCHY AS DEMOCRACY

by Wolf Jahn, Publ. by Anthony
d'Offay Gallery, London and Oktogon,
Munich

WITH GILBERT AND GEORGE
IN MOSCOW

by Daniel Farson
Publ. by Bloomsbury, London

THE COSMOLOGICAL PICTURES

Dual texts in English and Polish, Italian,
German, Hungarian, Dutch, Spanish by
Rudi Fuchs and Wojciech Markowski,
Published by Haags Gemeentemuseum,
The Hague

1992

NEW DEMOCRATIC PICTURES

Texts in English and Danish by Anders
Kold, Lars Morrell and Andrew Wilson
Publ. by Aarhus Kunstmuseum, Aarhus

1993

THE SINGING SCULPTURE

Texts by Carter Ratcliffe and Robert
Rosenblum, Publ. by Thames &
Hudson, London and Anthony McCall
Associates, New York

GILBERT & GEORGE
CHINA EXHIBITION

Texts by Wojciech Markowski, Norman
Rosenthal and interview with Andrew Wilson
Publ. by Gilbert & George, London /
Anthony d'Offay Gallery, London

1994

GILBERT & GEORGE:
RECENT WORKS

Publ. by Robert Miller Gallery,
New York

GILBERT & GEORGE

Text by Wolf Jahn. Publ. by Museo
d'Arte Moderna della Citta di Lugano

THE NAKED SHIT PICTURES

Text by Wolf Jahn. Publ. by Galerie
Rafael Jablonka, Cologne

SHITTY NAKED HUMAN WORLD

Text by Gilbert George,
Publ. by Wolfsburg Kunstmuseum

1995

THE NAKED SHIT PICTURES

Publ. by South London Gallery and
Anthony d'Offay Gallery, London

1996

THE NAKED SHIT PICTURES

Publ. by Stedelijk Museum, Amsterdam

GILBERT & GEORGE

Text by Danilo Eccher. Publ. by
Edizioni Charta, Milano /
Galleria d'Arte Moderna, Bologna

LOST DAY

Publ. by Oktagon Verlag, Köln (flick book)

'OH, THE GRAND OLD
DUKE OF YORK'

Publ. by Oktagon Verlag, Köln (flick book)

1997

THE FUNDAMENTAL PICTURES

Text by Robert Rosenblum,
Publ. by Alexander Roussos, London

GILBERT AND GEORGE –
ART FOR ALL 1971-1996

Texts by Robert Rosenblum and Sunihiro
Nonomura. Publ. by Sezon Museum of
Art, Tokyo

GILBERT & GEORGE – KONST

Publ. by Magasin 3, Stockholm

GILBERT & GEORGE

Interview by Martin Gayford. Publ. by
Musée d'Art Moderne de la Ville de Paris

THE WORDS OF
GILBERT & GEORGE

with Portraits of the Artists from 1968 to
1997. Publ. by Thames & Hudson in
association with Robert Violette Editions

1998

NEW TESTAMENTAL PICTURES

Text by Démosthène Davvetas, Publ. by
Galerie Thaddaeus Ropac, Paris

NEW TESTAMENTAL PICTURES

Texts by Achille Bonito Oliva, Mario
Codognato and Angela Tecce. Publ. by
Museo di Capodimonte, Napoli

1999

GILBERT & GEORGE A PORTRAIT

by Daniel Farson, Publ. by HarperCollins

GILBERT & GEORGE 1970-1997

Text by Øystein Ustvedt, Publ. by Astrup
Fearnley Museet for Moderne Kunst, Oslo

GILBERT & GEORGE 1986 – 1997

Interview by Wolf Jahn,
Publ. by Generalitat Valenciana

POSTAL SCULPTURES

1969

THE EASTER CARDS
SOUVENIR HYDE PARK WALK
A MESSAGE FROM THE SCULPTORS (DATED 1970)
ALL MY LIFE
1969/70 NEW DECADENT ART

1970

THE SADNESSS IN OUR ART

1971

THE LIMERICKS

1972

1ST POST-CARD
2ND POST-CARD

1973

THE PINK ELEPHANTS

1975

THE RED BOXERS

MAGAZINE SCULPTURES

1969

THE WORDS OF THE SCULPTORS

Jam Magazine, pp. 43-47, Autumn

1970

THE SHIT AND THE CUNT
WITH US IN NATURE

Studio International, pp. 218-221, May
Kunstmarkt, Cologne (catalogue)

1971

TWO TEXT PAGES
DESCRIBING OUR POSITION

The Sunday Times Magazine,
January 10

1972

THERE WERE TWO YOUNG MEN

Studio International, pp. 220-221, May

1973

BALLS

Avalanche, pp. 26-33, Summer-Fall

WORKS IN EDITION

1970

THE WORLDS OF THE SCULPTORS (edition 35)
WALKING VIEWING RELAXING (edition 13)
TO BE WITH ART IS ALL WE ASK (edition 9)
TWO TEXT PAGES DESCRIBING OUR POSITION (edition 19)

1971

THE TEN SPEECHES (edition 10)
THE EIGHT LIMERICKS (edition 25)

1972

MORNING LIGHT ON ART FOR ALL (edition 12)
GREAT EXPECTATIONS (edition 12)
AS USED BY THE SCULPTORS (edition 30)

1973

RECLINING DRUNK (edition 200)

1976

THE RED SCULPTURE (edition 100)

1979

FIRST BLOSSOM (edition 50)

1993

THE SINGING SCULPTURE 1969-91 (edition 20)

FILMS BY GILBERT & GEORGE

1970

THE NATURE OF OUR LOOKING (edition 4)

1972

GORDON'S MAKES US DRUNK (edition 25)
IN THE BUSH (edition 25)
PORTRAIT OF THE ARTISTS AS YOUNG MEN (edition 25)

1981

THE WORLD OF
GILBERT & GEORGE

Produced by Philip Haas for the
Arts Council of Great Britain (70 minutes)

FILMS ABOUT GILBERT & GEORGE

1984

GILBERT & GEORGE

South of Watford, ITV (with Ben Elton)

1986

RECONTRE A LONDRES

Vidéo Londres, Michel Burcel, France

GILBERT & GEORGE

La Estación de Perpiñàn, TVE, Spain

1991

THE RED SCULPTURE

Sonnabend / Castelli, New York

1991

THE SINGING SCULPTURE
BY GILBERT & GEORGE

Produced and directed by Philip Haas
for Sonnabend / Methodact

1992

GILBERT & GEORGE:
DAYTRIPPING

Produced and directed by Ian McDonald
for Anglia Television

1997

THE SOUTH BANK SHOW
WITH GILBERT & GEORGE

Produced and directed by Gerry Fox for
London Weekend Television

LIVING SCULPTURE PRESENTATIONS

1969

OUR NEW SCULPTURE	St. Martin's School of Art, London
READING FROM A STICK	Geffrye Museum, London
OUR NEW SCULPTURE	Royal College of Art, London
OUR NEW SCULPTURE	Camberwell School of Art, London
UNDERNEATH THE ARCHES	Slade School of Fine Art, London
SCULPTURE IN THE 60'S	Royal College of Art (with Bruce McLean)
IN THE UNDERWORLD	St. Martin's School of Art (with Bruce McLean)
IMPRESARIOS OF THE ART WORLD	Hanover Grand Preview Theatre (with Bruce McLean)
MEETING SCULPTURES	various locations, London
THE MEAL RIPLEY	Bromley, Kent (with David Hockney)
METALISED HEADS	Studio International Office, London
TELLING A STORY	The Lyceum Ballroom, London
THE SINGING SCULPTURE	National Jazz & Blues Festival, London
A LIVING SCULPTURE	at the opening of 'When Attitudes Become Form' ICA, London
UNDERNEATH THE ARCHES	Cable Street, London
POSING THE STAIRS	Stedelijk Museum, Amsterdam

1970

3 LIVING PIECES	BBC Studios, Bristol
LECTURE SCULPTURE	Museum of Modern Art, Oxford
LECTURE SCULPTURE	Leeds Polytechnic, Leeds
UNDERNEATH THE ARCHES	Kuntsthalle, Dusseldorf
UNDERNEATH THE ARCHES	Kunstverein, Hannover
UNDERNEATH THE ARCHES	Block Gallery Forum Theatre, Berlin
POSING PIECE	Art & Project, Amsterdam
POSING PIECE	Konrad Fischer Gallery, Dusseldorf
UNDERNEATH THE ARCHES	Kunstverein, Recklinghausen
UNDERNEATH THE ARCHES	Heiner Friedrich Gallery, Munich
UNDERNEATH THE ARCHES	Kunstverein, Nuremberg
UNDERNEATH THE ARCHES	Wurttembergischer Kunstverein, Stuttgart
UNDERNEATH THE ARCHES	Museum of Modern Art, Turin
UNDERNEATH THE ARCHES	Sonja Henie Niels Onstad Foundation, Oslo
UNDERNEATH THE ARCHES	Stadsbiblioteket Lyngby, Copenhagen
STANDING SCULPTURE	Folker Skulima Gallery, Berlin

UNDERNEATH THE ARCHES	Gegenverkehr, Aachen
UNDERNEATH THE ARCHES	Heiner Friedrich Gallery, Cologne
UNDERNEATH THE ARCHES	Kunstverein, Krefeld
UNDERNEATH THE ARCHES	Nigel Greenwood Gallery, London

1971

UNDERNEATH THE ARCHES	Garden Stores Louise, Brussels
UNDERNEATH THE ARCHES	for BBC play 'The Cowshed', London
UNDERNEATH THE ARCHES	Sonnabend Gallery, New York

1972

UNDERNEATH THE ARCHES	Kuntsmuseum, Lucerne
UNDERNEATH THE ARCHES	L'Attico Gallery, Rome

1973

UNDERNEATH THE ARCHES	National Gallery of New South Wales, Sydney (a John Kaldor Project)
UNDERNEATH THE ARCHES	National Gallery of Victoria, Melbourne, (a John Kaldor Project)

1975

SHAO LIN MARTIAL ARTS	Collegiate Theatre, London (Film Presentation)
THE RED SCULPTURE	Art Agency, Tokyo

1976

THE RED SCULPTURE	Sonnabend Gallery, New York
THE RED SCULPTURE	Konrad Fischer Gallery, Dusseldorf
THE RED SCULPTURE	Lucio Amelio Gallery, Naples

1977

THE RED SCULPTURE	Sperone Gallery, Rome
THE RED SCULPTURE	Robert Self Gallery, London
THE RED SCULPTURE	Sperone Fischer, Basel Art Fair
THE RED SCULPTURE	MTL Gallery, Brussels
THE RED SCULPTURE	Museum van Hedendaagse Kunst, Ghent
THE RED SCULPTURE	Stedelijk Museum, Amsterdam

1991

THE SINGING SCULPTURE	Sonnabend Gallery, New York

Acknowledgements

Numerous individuals have given their time and energy to this project, and in particular we wish to record our thanks to the following:

Dudley Allison, Blonski|Heard Associates, Fionnuala Boyd, Don Brown, Carol Burgess, Ruth Charity, Lee Farmer, Ealan Wingate and Lisa Kim of the Gagosian Gallery, Kirsten Gibbs, Emma Gregory, Robert de Grey, Gilbert & George, Tim Hill, Nigel Howse, Ronny Kimbell, John King, Dominic Legge, Michael Lynas & Milton Keynes Theatre staff, Sue Mackenzie Gray, Brian Meek, Natasha Messenger, Jane Morgan, Chris Murray, John & Sue Napleton, Edna Read Neal, John Newling, Raymond O'Daly, Antonia Payne, Andrew Peck, Jan Riordan, Alexander Roussos, Christina Rowe, Pauline Scott-Garrett, Julia Seal, Pat Smith, Ian Smithie, Katharine Sorensen, Sir John Southby, Eileen Sparrow, Sir Peter & Lady Thompson, Roger Tomlinson and Alan Ward

Stephen Snoddy, Director, MK G

Capital Funding

Milton Keynes Theatre & Gallery Company acknowledges support from The National Lottery through the Arts Council of England, Milton Keynes Council and English Partnerships.

Revenue Funding

Milton Keynes Gallery acknowledges support from Milton Keynes Council and Southern Arts.

Capital Appeal Corporate Sponsors

Abbey National Charitable Trust
Abbeygate Developments Ltd
Adam Equipment Co Ltd
Advance Catering Equipment
Alpine Electronics of UK
Aquabar Ltd
Argos Distributors Limited
ASK Europe Plc
Association of Milton Keynes Hoteliers
Balzers Ltd
BMH Construction (Clifton) Ltd
Barclays Bank plc
PJ Carey (Contractors) Ltd
Capital and Regional Properties plc
Child Base Ltd
City Truck Group Ltd
Cornhill Insurance
Brian Currie Milton Keynes
dataCulture Limited
Denton Hall
Douglas Duff
DRS plc
Electronic Data Systems Ltd
East Midlands Electricity
Exel Logistics
Fennemores
Franklins Solicitors
The Gas Light & Coke Company
Gazeley Properties Ltd
Genesis Homes
Hammond & Dummer Ltd
Hays Distribution
Holophane Lighting Ltd
Howes Percival
HSBC plc
ING Real Estate
Initial City Link
Jaipur Restaurant
John Lewis Milton Keynes
Kemble & Co
Kimbell & Co
KingsMead Homes
Kirkby & Diamond
KPMG
Laing Limited
Lambert Smith Hampton
Lloyds TSB Group plc

David Lock Associates Ltd
Lundbeck Ltd
Lynx Data Cabling
Marks & Spencer plc
Marshall Amplification plc
Mazars Neville Russell
McCann Homes Ltd
Mercer & Hole
Merchants Ltd
Miletree Construction
Milton Keynes Parks Trust Ltd
Milton Keynes Shopping Centre Association
Milton Keynes Preparatory School
Minolta (UK) Ltd
Mobil Oil Co Ltd
Municipal Cleansing Services Ltd
NatWest Corporate Banking Services
Niftylift Ltd
ntl:
Peerless Hill Partnership
Pell Frischmann Group Ltd
Personal Assurance Plc
Pharmacia & Upjohn Ltd
Power Internet Ltd
PricewaterhouseCoopers
Routeco plc
Sir Peter Thompson
Stone & Webster
Tensator Ltd
The Commission for the New Towns
the fifth dimension
The Henry Moore Foundation
The Management Technology Partnership
The Milton Keynes Citizen Newspaper
The Open University
The Powell Foundation
The Saxon Clinic
Tibbett & Britten Group plc
Trilogy Computers Limited
Turney Landscapes Ltd
Unisys Ltd
Warren Thomas & Company
Waterline Ltd
Wayside Group
Willowbrite Ltd
Wilson Bowden plc
Workplace Systems plc
Yamaha-Kemble Music (UK) Ltd